The Day of Doom

OR A POETICAL DESCRIPTION OF THE GREAT

AND LAST JUDGMENT

with other poems

by MICHAEL WIGGLESWORTH

Edited with an introduction

by KENNETH B. MURDOCK

The Day of Doom

OR A POETICAL DESCRIPTION OF THE GREAT

AND LAST JUDGMENT

with other poems

by MICHAEL WIGGLESWORTH

Edited with an introduction

by KENNETH B. MURDOCK

With drawings adapted from early New England gravestones
by WANDA GÁG

NEW YORK / RUSSELL & RUSSELL

1966

FIRST PUBLISHED IN 1929
REISSUED, 1966, BY RUSSELL & RUSSELL
A DIVISION OF ATHENEUM HOUSE, INC.
BY ARRANGEMENT WITH THE SPIRAL PRESS
L.C. CATALOG CARD NO: 66—13246

PRINTED IN THE UNITED STATES OF AMERICA

Introduction

One night in 1653 Michael Wigglesworth dreamed of the "dreadful day of judgement," and "was thereby exceedingly awakened in spirit . . . to follow God with tears and cries." Nearly nine years later he finished a poem on the subject of his dream. *The Day of Doom* was printed in 1662, and at once achieved extraordinary success. "It pleased the Lord," Wigglesworth declared, "to give vent for my books and greater acceptance than I could have expected: so that of eighteen hundred there were scarce any unsold (or but few) at the year's end." There were then in New England probably about thirty-six thousand settlers, and in all the English colonies in the limits of the present United States, about eighty-five thousand. A copy of *The Day of Doom* was sold for one out of every twenty persons in New England, or one out of every forty-five in the colonies as a whole. A book which did as well to-day in relation to the population would break records as a "best seller," for it would have a sale of four hundred thousand in New England alone and of more than two and a half million in the nation. Nor was the popularity of Wigglesworth's verses but a flash in the pan.

They were speedily reprinted; there were probably four American editions before 1701, and certainly two London editions. 1701, 1711, 1715, 1751, 1774, 1777, 1811, and 1828, saw new appearances of the book; and in 1867, though it was then considered merely a curious literary relic, it was published by the American News Co. in New York. A friend of Wigglesworth suggested in 1705 that *The Day of Doom* would continue to be read till the last dread day itself, and though he was no doubt too sanguine there have been for more than two hundred years persons willing to print — and that implies someone willing to read — the lines which Michael Wigglesworth dedicated to the service of God.

III

Wigglesworth is remembered to-day only for what he wrote, but he was once loved as the man, and respected as the divine. Outwardly his career was uneventful. Born in England he came to Massachusetts in 1638 when he was not quite seven. He graduated from Harvard, taught there — worrying over the defects, intellectual and moral, of his pupils, and characteristically blaming himself no less than the "spirit of unbridled licentiousness" of the younger generation — got a smattering of medical learning, travelled as far from Cambridge as Connecticut, and once even found his way to Bermuda, and, soon after 1655 settled regularly as minister at Malden. His health failed, and "for some whole sevens of years" he could not preach. He turned to writing and in the foreword "To the Christian Reader," in *The Day of Doom*, he explains his position. Sick (and eager to refute those who asserted that his only malady was bred of his own fancy) he tells how, barred from the pulpit, he still finds

> "more true delight
> In serving of the Lord,
> Than all the good things upon Earth,
> Without it, can afford."

The Day of Doom, a "little piece," written by "a fool,"

> "as frail
> Impatient a Creature
> As most that tread upon the ground,"

was composed for God's "dear sake" by one who, "wanting other means," would "advantage" Him with his pen. In a similar spirit he wrote his other verses — *God's Controversy with New England* and *Meat Out of the Eater*.

He married three times — once, be it remembered in the teeth of protests from his clerical brethren who believed the lady of his choice unworthy of him in education and birth. He became a Fellow of Harvard College, and he continued, in spite of his illness, as minister at Malden. Eventually his affliction passed, and after "near twenty years almost buried alive" he was able to shoulder his work again. In his last years, "a little feeble shadow of a man, beyond seventy," he preached "usually twice or thrice in a week," and gave himself to "visiting and comforting the afflicted; encouraging the private meetings; catechizing the children of the flock; and managing the government of the church; and attending the sick, not only as a pastor, but as a physician, too; and this not only in his own town, but also in all those of the vicinity."

The outlines of his character are clear enough in his diaries and the comments of his friends. He was no hypocrite, no smug believer in his own salvation delighting in threatening others with the wrath to come. "Free from cant, conscientious even to morbidness, perpetually praying and struggling against pride and what he regarded as his besetting sins, aspiring after a religious state altogether unattainable, ever faithful to the extent of his strength and capacity, and fearful lest his interest in his pupils and others should steal away his heart from God, in whom his trust was so strong as to appear almost ridiculous to men who regard the Almighty as quite indifferent to their fortunes," – this was John L. Sibley's estimate of Wigglesworth, printed in 1873. That it was not overdrawn his diary proves. "My proneness to satisfy my soul in my study's or pupils' progress, or anything without God, is," he wrote, "the daily fear of my soul, the secret pitfall . . . that fills me with fear, so that I dare not go on sometimes in my studies as my over eager spirit would carry me without recalling myself to muse of the things of God . . . I am much perplexed about my pupils and how to carry to them, but I cannot obtain a broken heart for the same carriages in myself to my God." Beginning to feel more confidence in his own virtue, he pulls himself up sharply by suggesting that he acts from fear of punishment and not from love for God. And, poor man, hearing someone "speaking in commendation of seasonable laughter and merriment, as that which may be a means to recreate one's tired spirits," he decides: "My heart is so naught that should I give it liberty . . . I have cause to fear lest I should take pleasure for itself, without reference to health . . . Let me rather live a melancholy life all my days, than by merriment run into a course of provoking my God." There is one line in his diary more pathetic still: "I am afraid lest I desire health more than holiness."

For Wigglesworth to be a Christian meant, in Herbert's phrase, "a good strife." His love of study for its own sake, his leanings toward merriment, his perpetual longing for health, all must be put down that he might set above them God and what he conceived of as holiness. Repellent as seems the code he revered, in his dogged struggle to live up to it, terrified lest he fail, distrustful of his success, tortured by visions of an eternity of punishment, and at war with his quite natural and quite innocent impulses, he is more than a country minister, a prey to nervous depression — he becomes instead a heroic figure, of modest proportions but still recognizable as one who dared and suffered for an ideal.

Wigglesworth's artistic yearnings do not find anything like full scope in *The Day of Doom*, nor are the qualities which made him loved completely displayed in it. Critic after critic has found in the little volume only brimstone and bad verse. Why, then, its popularity?

So far as Wigglesworth's own day is concerned, the answer is easy. The poem presented what was then sound doctrine in a form which, if not satisfying to the most critical in matters of style, was at least in a familiar tradition of popular verse. For a century after 1662 there were many Americans for whom Wigglesworth's theology was still law, and they turned to the poem, as their fathers had done, for the instruction it

VI

contained. They did not bring to it a resolute determination to measure it by the highest canons of poetry; they knew that to apply purely literary criteria was beside the point. The very man who thought so highly of *The Day of Doom* that he predicted immortality for it, found nothing to praise in it on the score of art. Its author, he said, "proposed the edification of such readers as are for truths dressed up in a plain meter," and among such readers the verses had their "acceptance and advantage." It is not a great poem and never was, nor is there any reason to suppose that the author or his most enthusiastic readers ever supposed it to be. They relished its piety and were not disturbed because Wigglesworth was not free to obey such artistic promptings as he had. He was handicapped on the one hand by his allegiance to the letter of the Bible as expounded by his school of theology, and on the other by his knowledge of his audience. He might conceivably have created an emotionally moving picture of Doomsday, full of color and compact of poetry, but had he done so he must have shot above his readers' heads. In an unpublished essay on "Eloquence" he remarked: "He is the best artist who can most clearly and familiarly communicate his thoughts to the meanest capacity," and to this standard, at least, he lived up. His ballad measure too often seems absurdly unsuited to the theme, but it was grateful to the ears of the relatively unlettered New Englander whom he wanted to reach. Blank verse or well-turned couplets might have struck his audience as difficult or unfamiliar, but the colonists knew ballads, had probably read or heard more than one of the English Day of Judgment ballads, and so found no obstacle of form set up in the way of their ready comprehension of Wigglesworth's stanzas. They at least were not offended by having the speeches of Christ and of human souls before the throne uttered in the jog-trot measure of *The Nut-Brown Maid.*

According to some commentators *The Day of Doom* is chiefly distinguished by its sulphurousness, the cruelty of its doctrine, and its harping on the horrors of Hell. Wigglesworth's portrayal of God has in the eyes of some critics sufficed to give the poem unpleasant eminence among works of its kind. According to Moses Coit Tyler, the author "with entire unconsciousness, attributes to the Divine Being a character the most execrable and loathsome to be met with, perhaps, in any literature, Christian or pagan." Yet the theology of *The Day of Doom* is in many respects that of Augustine, and, in most, that of Calvin, of certain Elizabethan bishops, of John Bunyan, and of thousands of English men and women throughout the seventeenth century. *The Day of Doom* smells no more strongly of brimstone than the utterances or writings of hundreds of others, in New England and out of it, during Wigglesworth's life, and before and after it.

Even the unhappy children of *The Day of Doom* are not Wigglesworth's own creations. Any good Calvinist would have found it hard to think of their situation as better than that which Wigglesworth gives them in "the easiest room in Hell." Other writers, to be sure, liked to evade the question of infant damnation and to express no convictions about it, but Richard Baxter writing in England in 1673 lists thirteen views of the problem held by theologians of various creeds, and but one of the thirteen outlaws Wigglesworth's belief that some infants were damned. Repulsive as is the picture of the wretched children in *The Day of Doom*, it is the picture which countless Christians of different sects in many periods must have drawn had they faced, as Wigglesworth did, the task of revealing all the imagined details of the last judgment. And, finally, it is impossible to claim for *The Day of Doom* even the doubtful honor of depicting God in darker colors than those with which He is painted elsewhere. To be sure the Saviour does debate with miserable souls with a sprightly casuistry which, in view of their plight, seems brutal. To be sure He utters the sentence of damnation with a hint of relish which savors too strongly of joy in vengeance. But these things are true of the God of many another theologian and many another poet of Wigglesworth's century.

The Almighty of *The Day of Doom* is not a reflection of a single New Englander's rigors and fiercenesses but of a theological conception to which great groups of Christians for years brought assent. As Mr. Paul Elmer More puts it: "If you are going to depict an eternal hell, there's no use in being finicky about the benevolence of your deity" — a point which Wigglesworth grasped.

Anyone who cares to bask in the heat of theological bonfires will find *The Day of Doom* to his taste, but it is well to remember that it has no higher caloric value than, say, some sermons of John Donne, the Anglican poet, some pages of Edwards, the eighteenth century philosopher, or many a forgotten treatise or sermon from days before the Calvinists till days after the Victorians.

Denied the title of great poetry, shorn of its claim to peculiar infamy as a supreme example of theologic fire-breathing, it still does not deserve to be forgotten even now when it can move no one as it once moved the Puritan children who huddled beside the fire and became breathless with terror and awe as they spelled out its lines. For, after all, is there any document which sets forth more vividly what Calvinism meant for individuals, sects, nations, for years influenced in all the activities of life by its curious hold on the mind of man? Do many religious poems of England or America offer materials for portraits more dramatic than that of Michael Wigglesworth, sick, sensitive, gentle-natured, beset day and night by fears and hopes as to his future state, and haunted by an image of a just God condemning with cold logic myriad souls to a living death of torment?

It is, of course, as a historical document that *The Day of Doom* is most precious, but even the lover of literature alone may find rewards in reading it. He will, surely, if he is interested not only in the finished product of poetry but also in the raw material, and in books which, however unsuccessful, show the artist at work and waging his battle against the handicaps which warp and distort his expression. To try to select from *The Day of Doom* those stanzas which approach poetry (there are perhaps a few which attain it), to read the poem mindful of the author's triple problem, involving his audience, his zeal for edification, and his inexpert craftsmanship—these are ways of catching unexpected gleams from Wigglesworth's pages. *The Day of Doom* should be read as it was written, not as an isolated poem, but with the preface "To the Reader," and, especially, the "Postscript," for when it is so read its "hell-fire" is partly balanced by Wigglesworth's plea to men to repent and seek righteousness. The author himself constantly peeps out from behind the lines, and the poem goes far toward showing how one Calvinist managed to accept his theology without going mad. Wigglesworth conceived of God as supreme, and the embodiment of all truth, beauty, and love, whereas man was but a helpless dependent on divine bounty. For an individual human being to judge the Almighty by human standards would have been absurd. Wigglesworth had learned Francis Bacon's lesson: "The prerogative of God extendeth as well to the reason as to the will of man; so that as we are to obey his law though we find a reluctation in our will, so we are to believe his word though we find a reluctation in our reason."

The Day of Doom, moreover, can be read quite without concern for its historical or theological suggestiveness. Most of us in our more relaxed moments glow with a pleasant sense of our own virtue in reading anything which proves we are not as other men were. Or the poem may appeal simply because it is — or seems — comic. Even though there come at times an awkward hint that below the surface lies tragedy, it is diverting occasionally to read *The Day of Doom* simply as a curiosity and no more — a work in which a Divine Being conducts, in ballad measure, a logical debate with damned souls, and the terrors of the Pit are dealt with in the homely terms familiar to Puritan laymen two centuries ago. And for him who is ironically minded Wigglesworth and his verses may furnish a parable, wholesome to remember when idle speculations are in the air on such topics as the reasons for America's failures and successes in art and the true meaning of the words "American" and "democratic" when applied to literature.

To
The Christian Reader

Reader, I am a fool,
And have adventured
To play the fool this once for Christ,
The more his fame to spread.
If this my foolishness
Help thee to be more wise,
I have attained what I seek,
And what I onely prize.

Thou wonderest perhaps,
That I in Print appear,
Who to the Pulpit dwell so nigh,
Yet come so seldome there.
The God of Heaven knows
What grief to me it is,
To be with-held from Serving Christ:
No sorrow like to this.

This is the sorest pain
That I have felt or feel:
Yet have I stood some shocks that might
Make stronger Men to reel.
I find more true delight
In serving of my Lord,
Than all the good things upon Earth,
Without it, can afford.

And could my strength endure,
That work I count so dear;
Not all the Riches of Peru
Should hire me to forbear;
But I'm a Prisoner,
Under a heavy Chain:
Almighty God's afflicting hand,
Doth me perforce restrain.

Yet some (I know) do judge,
Mine inability,
To come abroad and do Christ's Work,
To be Melancholly;
And that I'm not so weak,
As I my self conceit,
But who, in other things have found
Me so conceited yet?

Or who of all my friends,
That have my tryals seen,
Can tell the time in seven years,
When I have dumpish been?
Some think my voice is strong,
Most times when I do Preach:
But ten days after what I feel
And suffer, few can reach.

My prisoned thoughts break forth,
When open'd is the door,
With greater force and violence,
And strain my voice the more.
But vainly do they tell,
That I am growing stronger,
Who hear me speak in half an hour,
Till I can speak no longer.

Some for, because they see not
My chearfulness to fail,
Nor that I am disconsolate,
Do think I nothing ail.
If they had born my griefs,
Their courage might have fail'd them,
And all the Town (perhaps) have known
(Once and again) what ail'd them.

But why should I complain
That have so good a God,
That doth mine heart with comfort fill,
Ev'n whilst I feel his Rod?
In God I have been strong,
When wearied and worn out;
And joy'd in him, when twenty woes
Assail'd me round about.

Nor speak I this to boast;
But make Apology
For mine own self, and answer those
That fail in Charity.
I am (alas) as frail,
Impatient a Creature,
As most that tread upon the ground,
And have as bad a nature.

3

Let God be magnify'd,
Whose everlasting strength
Upholds me under sufferings
Of more than ten years length.
Through whose Almighty pow'r
Although I am surrounded
With sorrows more than can be told,
Yet am I not confounded.

For his dear sake have I
This service undertaken,
For I am bound to honour Him,
Who hath not me forsaken.
I am a Debtor too,
Unto the sons of Men;
Whom wanting other means, I would
Advantage with my Pen.

I would, But (ah!) my strength,
When tried, proves so small,
That to the ground without effect,
My wishes often fall.
Weak heads, and hands, and states,
Great things cannot produce:
And therefore I this little Piece
Have publish'd for thine use.

Although the thing be small,
Yet my good will therein,
Is nothing less then if it had
A larger Volumn been.
Accept it then in Love,
And read it for thy good:
There's nothing in't can do thee hurt,
If rightly understood.

4

The God of Heaven grant
These Lines so well to speed,
That thou the things of thine own peace,
Through them may'st better heed,
And may'st be stirred up
To stand upon thy guard,
That Death and Judgment may not come,
And find thee unprepar'd.

Oh get a part in Christ,
And make the Judge thy Friend:
So shalt thou be assured of
A happy, glorious end.
Thus prayes thy real Friend,
And Servant for Christ's Sake,
Who had he strength would not refuse,
   More pains for thee to take.

MICHAEL WIGGLESWORTH

A Prayer unto Christ

THE JUDGE OF THE WORLD

O Dearest Dread, most glorious King,
I'le of thy justest Judgments sing:
Do thou my head and heart inspire,
To Sing aright, as I desire.
Thee, thee alone I'le invocate,
For I do much abominate
To call the Muses to mine aid:
Which is th' Unchristian use, and trade
Of some that Christians would be thought,
And yet they worship worse then nought.
Oh! what a deal of Blasphemy,
And Heathenish Impiety,
In Christian Poets may be found,
Where Heathen gods with praise are Crown'd,
They make Jehovah to stand by,
Till Juno, Venus, Mercury,

7

With *frowning* Mars, *and thundering* Jove
Rule Earth below, and Heaven above.
But I have learnt to pray to none,
Save unto God in Christ alone.
Nor will I laud, no, not in jest,
That which I know God doth detest.
I reckon it a damning evil
To give Gods Praises to the Devil.
Thou, Christ, *art he to whom I pray,*
Thy Glory fain I would display.
Oh! guide me by thy sacred Sprite
So to indite, and so to write,
That I thine holy Name may praise,
And teach the Sons of men thy wayes.

The Day of Doom

≺ 1 ≻

Still was the night, Serene and Bright,
  when all Men sleeping lay;
Calm was the season, and carnal reason
  thought so 'twould last for ay.
Soul, take thine ease, let sorrow cease,
  much good thou hast in store:
This was their Song, their Cups among,
  the Evening before.

The security of the World before Christs coming to judgment. Luke 12:19

≺ 2 ≻

Wallowing in all kind of sin,
  vile wretches lay secure:
The best of men had scarcely then
  their Lamps kept in good ure.
Virgins unwise, who through disguise
  amongst the best were number'd,
Had clos'd their eyes; yea, and the wise
  through sloth and frailty slumber'd.

Mat. 25:5

9

‹ 3 ›

Like as of old, when Men grow bold

Mat. 24:37, 38   Gods' threatnings to contemn,
Who stopt their Ear, and would not hear,
    when Mercy warned them:
But took their course, without remorse,
    till God began to powre
Destruction the World upon
    in a tempestuous showre.

‹ 4 ›

They put away the evil day,
    And drown'd their care and fears,
Till drown'd were they, and swept away
    by vengeance unawares:
1 *Thes.* 5:3   So at the last, whilst Men sleep fast
    in their security,
Surpriz'd they are in such a snare
    as cometh suddenly.

‹ 5 ›

The suddenness,   For at midnight brake forth a Light,
Majesty, &   which turn'd the night to day,
Terror of Christ's And speedily an hideous cry
appearing.   did all the world dismay.
Mat. 25:6   Sinners awake, their hearts do ake,
2 *Pet.* 3:10   trembling their loynes surprizeth;
Amaz'd with fear, by what they hear,
    each one of them ariseth.

‹ 6 ›

They rush from Beds with giddy heads,
    and to their windows run,
Viewing this light, which shines more bright
Mat. 24:29, 30   then doth the Noon-day Sun.
Straightway appears (they see't with tears)
    the Son of God most dread;
Who with his Train comes on amain
    To Judge both Quick and Dead.

10

Before his face the Heav'ns gave place,
    and Skies are rent asunder,   2 *Pet.* 3:10
With mighty voice, and hideous noise,
    more terrible than Thunder.
His brightness damps heav'ns glorious lamps
    and makes them hide their heads,
As if afraid and quite dismay'd,
    they quit their wonted steads.

Ye sons of men that durst contemn
    the Threatnings of Gods Word,
How cheer you now? your hearts, I trow,
    are thrill'd as with a sword.
Now Atheist blind, whose brutish mind
    a God could never see,
Dost thou perceive, dost now believe,
    that Christ thy Judge shall be?

Stout Courages, (whose hardiness
    could Death and Hell out-face)
Are you as bold now you behold
    your Judge draw near apace?
They cry, no, no: Alas! and wo!
    our Courage all is gone:
Our hardiness (fool hardiness)
    hath us undone, undone.

No heart so bold, but now grows cold
    and almost dead with fear:
No eye so dry, but now can cry,   *Rev.* 6:16
    and pour out many a tear.
Earths Potentates and pow'rful States,
    Captains and Men of Might
Are quite abasht, their courage dasht
    at this most dreadful sight.

Mean men lament, great men do rent
    their Robes, and tear their hair:
Mat. 24:30   They do not spare their flesh to tear
    through horrible despair.
All Kindreds wail: all hearts do fail:
    horror the world doth fill
With weeping eyes, and loud out-cries,
    yet knows not how to kill.

Rev. 6:15, 16   Some hide themselves in Caves and Delves,
    in places under ground:
Some rashly leap into the Deap,
    to scape by being drown'd:
Some to the Rocks (O sensless blocks!)
    and woody Mountains run,
That there they might this fearful sight,
    and dreaded Presence shun.

In vain do they to Mountains say,
    Fall on us, and us hide
From Judges ire, more hot than fire,
    for who may it abide?
No hiding place can from his Face,
    sinners at all conceal,
Whose flaming Eyes hid things doth 'spy,
    and darkest things reveal.

The Judge draws nigh, exalted high
Mat. 25:31   upon a lofty Throne,
Amidst the throng of Angels strong,
    lo, Israel's Holy One!
The excellence of whose presence
    and awful Majesty,
Amazeth Nature, and every Creature,
    doth more than terrify.

◄ 15 ►

The Mountains smoak, the Hills are shook,   *Rev.* 6:14
  the Earth is rent and torn,
As if she should be clean dissolv'd,
  or from the Center born.
The Sea doth roar, forsakes the shore,
  and shrinks away for fear;
The wild Beasts flee into the Sea,
  so soon as he draws near.

◄ 16 ►

Whose Glory bright, whose wondrous might,
  whose Power Imperial,
So far surpass whatever was
  in Realms Terrestrial;
That tongues of men (nor Angels pen)
  cannot the same express,
And therefore I must pass it by,
  lest speaking should transgress.

◄ 17 ►

Before his Throne a Trump is blown,   1 *Thes.* 4:16
  Proclaiming th' Day of Doom: *Resurrection*
Forthwith he cries, *Ye Dead arise,*   *of the Dead.*
  and unto Judgment come.   *John* 5:28, 29
No sooner said, but 'tis obey'd;
  Sepulchers open'd are:
Dead Bodies all rise at his call,
  and's mighty power declare.

◄ 18 ►

Both Sea and Land, at his Command,
  their Dead at once surrender:
The Fire and Air constrained are
  also their dead to tender.
The mighty word of this great Lord
  links Body and Soul together
Both of the Just, and the unjust,
  to part no more for ever.

*The living
Changed.*

The same translates, from Mortal states
    to Immortality,
All that survive, and be alive,
    i' th' twinkling of an eye:

Luk. 20:36
1 *Cor.* 15:52

That so they may abide for ay
    to endless weal or woe;
Both the Renate and Reprobate
    are made to dy no more.

*All brought
to Judgment.*
Mat. 24:31

His winged Hosts flie through all Coasts,
    together gathering
Both good and bad, both quick and dead,
    and all to Judgment bring.
Out of their holes those creeping Moles,
    that hid themselves for fear,
By force they take, and quickly make
    before the Judge appear.

2 *Cor.* 5:10
*The Sheep
separated from
the Goats.*
Mat. 25

Thus every one before the Throne
    of Christ the Judge is brought,
Both righteous and impious
    that good or ill had wrought.
A separation, and diff'ring station
    by Christ appointed is
(To sinners sad) 'twixt good and bad,
    'twixt Heirs of woe and bliss.

*Who are
Christ's Sheep.*
Mat. 5:10, 11

At Christ's right hand the Sheep do stand,
    his holy Martyrs, who
For his dear Name suffering shame,
    calamity and woe,
Like Champions stood, and with their Blood
    their testimony sealed;
Whose innocence without offence,
    to Christ their Judge appealed.

Next unto whom there find a room
    all Christ's afflicted ones,   *Heb.* 12:5,6,7
Who being chastised, neither despised
    nor sank amidst their groans:
Who by the Rod were turn'd to God,
    and loved him the more,
Not murmuring nor quarrelling
    when they were chast'ned sore.

Moreover, such as loved much,   *Luke* 7:41,47
    that had not such a tryal,
As might constrain to so great pain,
    and such deep self denyal:
Yet ready were the Cross to bear,
    when Christ them call'd thereto,
And did rejoyce to hear his voice,
    they're counted Sheep also.

Christ's Flock of Lambs there also stands,   *Joh.* 21:15
    whose Faith was weak, yet true;   *Mat.* 19:14
All sound Believers (Gospel receivers)   *Joh.* 3:3
    whose Grace was small, but grew:
And them among an Infant throng
    of Babes, for whom Christ dy'd;
Whom for his own, by wayes unknown
    to men, he sanctify'd.

All stand before their Saviour
    in long white Robes yclad,   *Rev.* 6:11
Their countenance full of pleasance,   *Phil.* 3:21
    appearing wondrous glad.
O glorious sight! Behold how bright
    dust heaps are made to shine,
Conformed so their Lord unto,
    whose Glory is Divine.

At Christ's left hand the Goats do stand,
    all whining hypocrites,
Who for self-ends did seem Christ's friends,
    but foster'd guileful sprites;
Who Sheep resembled, but they dissembled
    (their hearts were not sincere);
Who once did throng Christ's Lambs among,
    but now must not come near.

Apostates and Run-awayes,
    such as have Christ forsaken,
Of whom the Devil, with seven more evil,
    hath fresh possession taken:
Sinners in grain, reserv'd to pain
    and torments most severe:
Because 'gainst light they sinn'd with spight,
    are also placed there.

There also stand a num'rous band,
    that no Profession made

Of Godliness, nor to redress
    their wayes at all essay'd:
Who better knew, but (sinful Crew)
    Gospel and Law despised;
Who all Christ's knocks withstood like blocks
    and would not be advised.

Moreover, there with them appear
    a number, numberless

Of great and small, vile wretches all,
    that did Gods Law transgress:
Idolaters, false worshippers,
    Prophaners of Gods Name,
Who not at all thereon did call,
    or took in vain the same.

Blasphemers lewd, and Swearers shrewd,
  Scoffers at Purity,
That hated God, contemn'd his Rod,   *Exed.* 20:7, & 8
  and lov'd Security;
Sabbath-polluters, Saints persecuters,
  Presumptuous men and Proud,
Who never lov'd those that reprov'd;   2 *Thes.* 1:6, 8, 9
  all stand amongst this Crowd.

Adulterers and Whoremongers   *Heb.* 13:4
  were there, with all unchast: 1 *Cor.* 6:10
There Covetous, and Ravenous,
  that Riches got too fast:
Who us'd vile ways themselves to raise
  t'Estates and worldly wealth,
Oppression by, or Knavery,
  by force, or fraud, or stealth.

Moreover, there together were
  Children flagitious,
And Parents who did them undo   *Zach.* 5:3, 4
  by Nurture vicious.   *Gal.* 5:19, 20, 21
False-witness-bearers, and self-forswearers,
  Murd'rers, and Men of blood,
Witches, Inchanters, and Ale-house-haunters,
  beyond account there stood.

Their place there find all Heathen blind,
  that Natures light abused,
Although they had no tydings glad,   *Rom.* 2:13
  of Gospel-grace refused.
There stands all Nations and Generations
  of *Adam's* Progeny,
Whom Christ redeem'd not, who Christ esteem'd not,
  through Infidelity.

17

Act. 4:12

Who no Peace-maker, no Undertaker,
 to shrow'd them from Gods ire,
Ever obtain'd; they must be pained
 with everlasting fire.
These num'rous bands, wringing their hands
 and weeping, all stand there,
Filled with anguish, whose hearts do languish
 through self-tormenting fear.

≺ 36 ≻

Fast by them stand at Christ's left hand
 the Lion fierce and fell,
The Dragon bold, that Serpent old,
 that hurried Souls to Hell.

1 *Cor.* 6:3

There also stand, under command,
 Legions of Sprights unclean,
And hellish Fiends, that are no friends
 to God, nor unto Men.

≺ 37 ≻

With dismal chains, and strongest reins,
 like Prisoners of Hell,

Jude 6

They're held in place before Christ's face,
 till He their Doom shall tell.
These void of tears, but fill'd with fears,
 and dreadful expectation
Of endless pains, and scalding flames,
 stand waiting for Damnation.

≺ 38 ≻

All silence keep, both Goats and Sheep,
 before the Judge's Throne;

*The Saints
cleared &
justified.*

With mild aspect to his Elect
 then spake the Holy One:
My Sheep draw near, your Sentence hear,
 which is to you no dread,
Who clearly now discern, and know
 your sins are pardoned.

18

'Twas meet that ye should judged be,
   that so the world may spy
No cause of grudge, when as I Judge
   and deal impartially.
Know therefore all, both great and small,
   the ground and reason why
These Men do stand at my right hand,
   and look so chearfully.

2 Cor. 5:10
Eccles. 3:17
Joh. 3:18

These Men be those my Father chose
   before the worlds foundation,
And to me gave, that I should save
   from Death and Condemnation.
For whose dear sake I flesh did take,
   was of a Woman born,
And did inure my self t' indure,
   unjust reproach and scorn.

Joh. 17:6
Eph. 1:4

For them it was that I did pass
   through sorrows many one:
That I drank up that bitter Cup,
   which made me sigh and groan.
The Cross his pain I did sustain;
   yea more, my Fathers ire
I underwent, my Blood I spent
   to save them from Hell fire.

Rev. 1:5

Thus I esteem'd, thus I redeem'd
   all these from every Nation,
That they may be (as now you see)
   a chosen Generation.
What if ere-while they were as vile,
   and bad as any be,
And yet from all their guilt and thrall
   at once I set them free?

Eph. 2:1,3

Mat. 20:13,15
Rom. 9:20,21

My grace to one is wrong to none:
    none can Election claim,
Amongst all those their souls that lose,
    none can Rejection blame.
He that may chuse, or else refuse,
    all men to save or spill,
May this Man chuse, and that refuse,
    redeeming whom he will.

Isa. 53:4,5,11

But as for those whom I have chose
    Salvations heirs to be,
I underwent their punishment,
    and therefore set them free;
I bore their grief, and their relief
    by suffering procur'd,
That they of bliss and happiness
    might firmly be assur'd.

Acts. 13:48
Jam. 2:18
Heb. 12:7
Mat. 19:29

And this my grace they did imbrace,
    believing on my Name;
Which Faith was true, the fruits do shew
    proceeding from the same:
Their Penitence, their Patience,
    their Love and Self-denial
In suffering losses, and bearing Crosses,
    when put upon the tryal.

Their sin forsaking, their chearful taking
    my yoke, their Charity

1 Joh. 3:3
Mat. 25:39,40

Unto the Saints in all their wants,
    and in them unto me,
These things do clear, and make appear
    their Faith to be unfaigned,
And that a part in my desert
    and purchase they have gained.

Their debts are paid, their peace is made,
 their sins remitted are;
Therefore at once I do pronounce,
 and openly declare
That Heav'n is theirs, that they be Heirs
 of Life and of Salvation!
Nor ever shall they come at all
 to Death or to Damnation.

Isa. 53:11,12
Rom. 8:16,17,
33,34
John 3:18

Come, Blessed Ones, and sit on Thrones,
 Judging the World with me:
Come, and possess your happiness,
 and bought felicitie.
Henceforth no fears, no care, no tears,
 no sin shall you annoy,
Nor any thing that grief doth bring:
 Eternal Rest enjoy.

Luk. 22:29,30
Mat. 19:28

You bore the Cross, you suffered loss
 of all for my Names sake:
Receive the Crown that's now your own;
 come, and a Kingdom take.
Thus spake the Judge; the wicked grudge,
 and grind their teeth in vain;
They see with groans these plac't on Thrones
 which addeth to their pain:

Mat. 25:34
They are placed on
Thrones to joyn
with Christ in
judging the wicked.

That those whom they did wrong and slay,
 must now their judgment see!
Such whom they slighted, and once despighted,
 must now their Judges be!
Thus 'tis decreed, such is their meed,
 and guerdon glorious!
With Christ they sit, Judging is fit
 to plague the Impious.

1 *Cor.* 6:2

The wicked
brought to the Bar.
Rom. 2:3, 6, 11

The wicked are brought to the Bar,
    like guilty Malefactors,
That oftentimes of bloody Crimes
    and Treasons have been Actors.
Of wicked Men, none are so mean
    as there to be neglected:
Nor none so high in dignity,
    as there to be respected.

Rev. 6:15, 16
Isa. 30:33

The glorious Judge will priviledge
    nor Emperour, nor King:
But every one that hath mis-done
    doth into Judgment bring.
And every one that hath mis-done,
    the Judge impartially
Condemneth to eternal wo,
    and endless misery.

Thus one and all, thus great and small,
    the Rich as well as Poor,
And those of place as the most base,
    do stand the Judge before.
They are arraign'd, and there detain'd,
    before Christ's Judgment-seat
With trembling fear, their Doom to hear,
    and feel his angers heat.

Eccles. 11:9 &
12:14

There Christ demands at all their hands
    a strict and strait account
Of all things done under the Sun,
    whose number far surmount
Man's wit and thought: yet all are brought
    unto this solemn Tryal;
And each offence with evidence,
    so that there's no denial.

There's no excuses for their abuses,
   since their own Consciences
More proof give in of each Man's sin,
   than thousand Witnesses,
Though formerly this faculty
   had grosly been abused,
Men could it stifle, or with it trifle,
   when as it them accused.

≺ 56 ≻

Now it comes in, and every sin
   unto Mens charge doth lay:
It judgeth them, and doth condemn,
   though all the world say nay.
It so stingeth and tortureth,
   it worketh such distress,
That each Man's self against himself,
   is forced to confess.

≺ 57 ≻

It's vain, moreover, for Men to cover
   the least iniquity:
The Judge hath seen, and privy been
   to all their villany.
He unto light, and open sight
   the works of darkness brings:
He doth unfold both new and old,
   both known and hidden things.

Secret sins and
works of darkness
brought to light.
Psal. 139:2, 4,
12
Rom. 2:16

≺ 58 ≻

All filthy facts, and secret acts,
   however closly done,
And long conceal'd, are there reveal'd
   before the mid-day Sun.
Deeds of the night shunning the light,
   which darkest corners sought,
To fearful blame, and endless shame,
   are there most justly brought.

Eccles. 12:14

Mat. 12:36
Rom. 7:7

And as all facts and grosser acts,
 so every word and thought,
Erroneous notion, and lustful motion,
 are unto judgment brought,
No sin so small and trivial
 but hither it must come:
Nor so long past, but now at last
 it must receive a doom.

An account
demanded of all
their actions.
Joh. 5:40
& 3:19
Mat. 25:19, 27

At this sad season, Christ asks a Reason
 (with just Austerity)
Of Grace refused, of light abus'd
 so oft, so wilfully:
Of Talents lent by them mispent,
 and on their Lust bestown;
Which if improv'd, as it behov'd,
 Heav'n might have been their own!

Of times neglected, of means rejected,
 of God's long-suffering,

Rom. 2:4, 5

And Patience, to Penitence
 that sought hard hearts to bring.
Why Cords of love did nothing move
 to shame or to remorse?
Why warnings grave, and counsels, have
 nought chang'd their sinful course?

Why chastenings, and evil things,
 why judgments so severe

Isa. 1:5

Prevailed not with them a jot,
 nor wrought an awful fear?

Jer. 2:20

Why Promises of Holiness,
 and new Obedience,
They oft did make, but always brake
 the same, to God's offence?

24

◄ 63 ►

Why still Hell-ward, without regard,
    they boldly ventured,
And chose Damnation before Salvation,
    when it was offered:
Why sinful pleasures, and earthly treasures,
    like fools, they prized more
Than heav'nly wealth, Eternal health,
    and all Christ's Royal store.

John 3:19, 20
Prov. 8:36
Luk. 12:20, 21

◄ 64 ►

Why, when he stood off'ring his Blood
    to wash them from their sin,
They would embrace no saving Grace,
    but liv'd and dy'd therein?
Such aggravations, where no evasions,
    nor false pretences hold,
Exaggerate and cumulate
    guilt more than can be told.

Luk. 13:34
Joh. 5:40
& 15:22

◄ 65 ►

They multiply and magnify
    mens gross iniquities,
They draw down wrath (as Scripture saith)
    out of Gods treasuries.
Thus all their ways Christ open lays
    to men and Angels view,
And, as they were, makes them appear
    in their own proper hew.

◄ 66 ►

Thus he doth find of all Mankind,
    that stand at his left hand,
No Mothers Son, but hath mis-done,
    and broken God's Command.
All have transgrest, even the best,
    and merited God's wrath
Unto their own perdition,
    and everlasting scath.

Rom. 3:10, 12

25

Rom. 6:23

Earths dwellers all, both great and small,
    have wrought iniquity,
And suffer must, for it is just,
    Eternal misery.
Amongst the many there come not any,
    before the Judge's face,
That able are themselves to clear,
    of all this cursed race.

Nevertheless, they all express,
    Christ granting liberty,
What for their way they have to say,
    how they have liv'd, and why.

*Hypocrites plead
for themselves*

They all draw near, and seek to clear
    themselves by making pleas;
There Hypocrites, false hearted wights,
    do make such pleas as these:

Lord, in thy Name, and by the same,
    we Devils dispossest,

Mat. 7:21, 22,
23

We rais'd the dead, and ministred
    succour to the distrest.
Our painful teaching, and pow'rful preaching
    by thine own wondrous might,
Did throughly win to God from sin
    many a wretched wight.

*The judge reply-
eth.* Joh. 6:70
1 *Cor.* 9:27

All this, quoth he, may granted be,
    and your case little better'd,
Who still remain under a chain,
    and many irons fetter'd.
You that the dead have quickened,
    and rescu'd from the grave,
Your selves were dead, yet never ned,
    a Christ your Souls to save.

You that could preach, and others teach
  what way to life doth lead;
Why were you slack to find that track,   *Rom.* 2:19:21,
  and in that way to tread?   22,23
How could you bear to see or hear
  of others freed at last,
From Satan's pawes, whilst in his jawes
  your selves were held more fast?

Who though you knew Repentance true,   Joh. 9:41
  and Faith in my great Name,
The only mean to quit you clean,
  from punishment and blame,
Yet took no pain true Faith to gain,   *Rev.* 2:21,22
  such as might not deceive,
Nor would repent, with true intent,
  your evil deeds to leave.

His Masters will how to fulfill
  the servant that well knew,
Yet left undone his duty known,   *Luk.* 12:47
  more plagues to him are due.   *Mat.* 11:21,22,
You against light perverted right;   24
  wherefore it shall be now
For *Sidon* and for *Sodoms* Land
  more easie than for you.

But we have in thy presence been,   *Another plea of*
  say some, and eaten there.   *hypocrites.*
Did we not eat thy Flesh for meat,   *Luk.* 13:26
  and feed on heavenly Cheer?
Whereon who feed shall never need,
  as thou thy self dost say,
Nor shall they dy eternally,
  but live with Christ for ay.

We may alledge, thou gav'st a pledge
    of thy dear love to us
In Wine and Bread, which figured
    thy Grace bestowed thus.
Of strengthning Seals, of sweetest Meals,
    have we so oft partaken;
And shall we be cast off by thee,
    and utterly forsaken?

Is Answered.
Luk. 13:27
Mat. 22:12

To whom the Lord thus in a word
    returns a short reply,
I never knew any of you
    that wrought iniquity.
You say y'have been my Presence in;
    but friends, how came you there
With Raiment vile that did defile
    and quite disgrace my Cheer?

Durst you draw near without due fear
    unto my holy Table?
Durst you prophane, and render vain
    so far as you were able,
Those Mysteries? which whoso prize
    and carefully improve
Shall saved be undoubtedly,
    and nothing shall them move.

How durst you venture, bold guests, to enter
    in such a sordid hew,

1 *Cor.* 11:27, 29

Amongst my guests, unto those Feasts
    that were not made for you?
How durst you eat for spiritual meat
    your bane, and drink damnation,
Whilst by your guile you rendred vile
    so rare and great Salvation?

Your fancies fed on heav'nly Bread,
   your hearts fed on some Lust:
You lov'd the Creature more than th' Creator,
   your Souls clave to the dust.   *Mat.* 6:21, 24
And think you by Hypocrisie,   *Rom.* 1:25
   and cloaked Wickedness,
To enter in, laden with sin,
   to lasting happiness?

≺ 80 ≻

This your excuse shews your abuse   1 *Cor.* 11:27, 29
   of things ordain'd for good;
And doth declare you guilty are
   of my dear Flesh and Blood.
Wherefore those Seals and precious Meals
   you put so much upon
As things divine, they seal and sign
   you to Perdition.

≺ 81 ≻

Then forth issue another Crew
   (those being silenced)
Who drawing nigh to the most High   *Another sort of*
   adventure thus to plead: *hypocrites make*
We sinners were, say they, it's clear,   *their pleas.*
   deserving Condemnation:
But did not we rely on thee,
   O Christ, for whole Salvation?

≺ 82 ≻

We did believe and oft receive
   thy gracious promises:
We took great care to get a share   *Act.* 8:13
   in endless happiness.   *Isa.* 58:2, 3
We pray'd and wept, we Fast-dayes kept, *Heb.* 64:5
   lewd ways we did eschew:
We joyful were thy Word to hear;
   we form'd our lives anew.

We thought our sin had pard'ned been;
   that our Estate was good,
Our debts all paid, our peace well made,
   our Souls wash'd with thy Blood.

2 Pet. 2:20

Lord, why dost thou reject us now,
   who have not thee rejected,
Nor utterly true sanctity
   and holy life neglected.

The Judge
uncaseth them.

The Judge incensed at their pretenced
   self-vanting Piety,
With such a look as trembling strook
   into them, made reply;

John. 2:24, 25

O impudent, impenitent,
   and guileful generation!
Think you that I cannot descry
   your hearts abomination?

You nor receiv'd, nor yet believ'd
   my Promises of Grace;

Joh. 6:64

Nor were you wise enough to prize
   my reconciled Face:

Psal. 50:16
Mat. 15:26

But did presume that to assume
   which was not yours to take,
And challenged the Childrens bread,
   yet would not sin forsake.

Rev. 3:17

Being too bold you laid fast hold,
   where int'rest you had none,
Your selves deceiving by your believing,
   all which you might have known,

Mat. 13:20

You ran away, but ran astray,
   with Gospel-promises,
And perished; being still dead
   in sins and trespasses.

How oft did I Hypocrisie
    and Hearts deceit unmask
Before your sight, giving you light   *Mat.* 6:2, 4, 24
    to know a Christians task?   *Jer.* 8:5, 6, 7, 8
But you held fast unto the last
    your own Conceits so vain;
No warning could prevail, you would
    your own Deceits retain.

As for your care to get a share
    in bliss; the fear of Hell,
And of a part in endless smart,   *Psal.* 78:34, 35,
    did thereunto compel.   36, 37
Your holiness and ways redress,
    such as it was, did spring
From no true love to things above,
    but from some other thing.

You pray'd and wept, you Fast-days kept;   *Zach.* 7:5, 6
    but did you this to me?   *Isa.* 58:3, 4
No, but for sin, you sought to win,   1 *Sam.* 15:13, 21
    the greater libertie.   *Isaiah* 1:11, 15
For all your vaunts, you had vile haunts,
    for which your Consciences
Did you alarm, whose voice to charm
    you us'd these practices.

Your Penitence, your diligence
    to Read, to Pray, to Hear,   *Mat.* 6:2, 5
Were but to drown'd the clamorous sound *John* 5:44
    of Conscience in your ear.
If light you lov'd, vain glory mov'd
    your selves therewith to store,
That seeming wise, men might you prize,
    and honour you the more.

Thus from your selves unto your selves,
   your duties all do tend:
And as self-love the wheels doth move,
   so in self-love they end.
Thus Christ detects their vain projects,
   and close Impiety,
And plainly shews that all their shows
   were but Hypocrisy.

Zach. 7:15, 6
Hos. 10:1

Civil honest mens
pleas.
Luk. 18:11

Then were brought nigh a Company
   of Civil honest Men,
That lov'd true dealing, and hated stealing,
   ne'r wrong'd their Bretheren;
Who pleaded thus, Thou knowest us
   that we were blameless livers;
No Whoremongers, no Murderers,
   no quarrellers nor strivers.

Idolaters, Adulterers,
   Church-robbers we were none,
Nor false-dealers, no couzeners,
   but paid each man his own.
Our way was fair, our dealing square,
   we were no wastful spenders,
No lewd toss-pots, no drunken sots,
   no scandalous offenders.

We hated vice, and set great price,
   by vertuous conversation:
And by the same we got a name,
   and no small commendation.

1 *Sam.* 15:22

Gods Laws express that righteousness,
   is that which he doth prize;
And to obey, as he doth say,
   is more than sacrifice.

Thus to obey, hath been our way;
  let our good deeds, we pray,
Find some regard and some reward
  with thee, O Lord, this day.
And whereas we transgressors be,   *Eccles.* 7:20
  of *Adam's* Race were none,
No not the best, but have confest
  themselves to have mis-done.

Then answered unto their dread,   *Are taken off &*
  the Judge: True Piety   *rendred invalid.*
God doth desire and eke require   *Deut.* 10:12
  no less than honesty.   *Tit.* 2:12
Justice demands at all your hands   *Jam.* 2:10
  perfect Obedience:
If but in part you have come short,
  that is a just offence.

On Earth below, where men did ow
  a thousand pounds and more,
Could twenty pence it recompence?
  could that have clear'd the score?
Think you to buy felicity
  with part of what's due debt?
Or for desert of one small part,
  the whole should off be set?

And yet that part, whose great desert
  you think to reach so far
For your excuse, doth you accuse,
  and will your boasting mar.   *Luk.* 18:11,14
However fair, however square,
  your way and work hath been,
Before mens eyes, yet God espies
  iniquity therein.

1 Sam. 16:7
2 Chron. 25:2

God looks upon th' affection
   and temper of the heart;
Not only on the action,
   and the external part.
Whatever end vain men pretend,
   God knows the verity;
And by the end which they intend
   ˜˜their words and deeds doth try.

Heb. 11:6

Without true Faith, the Scripture saith
   God cannot take delight
In any deed, that doth proceed
   from any sinful wight.

1 Cor. 13:1, 2, 3

And without love all actions prove
   but barren empty things.
Dead works they be, and vanitie,
   the which vexation brings.

Nor from true faith, which quencheth wrath,
   hath your obedience flown:
Nor from true love, which wont to move
   Believers, hath it grown.
Your argument shews your intent,
   in all that you have done:
You thought to scale Heav'ns lofty Wall
   by Ladders of your own.

Rom. 10:3

Your blinded spirit, hoping to merit
   by your own Righteousness,
Needed no Saviour, but your behaviour,
   and blameless carriages;
You trusted to what you could do,
   and in no need you stood:
Your haughty pride laid me aside,
   and trampled on my Blood.

34

All men have gone astray, and done,
　　that which Gods Laws condemn:
But my Purchase and offered Grace
　　all men did not contemn.
The *Ninevites*, and *Sodomites*,
　　had no such sin as this:
Yet as if all your sins were small,
　　you say, All did amiss.

Rom. 9:30,32
Mat. 11:23, 24
& 12:41

Again you thought and mainly sought
　　a name with men t'acquire;
Pride bare the Bell, that made you swell,
　　and your own selves admire.
Mean fruit it is, and vile, I wiss,
　　that springs from such a root:
Vertue divine and genuine
　　wonts not from pride to shoot.

Mat. 6:5

Such deeds as your are worse than poor;
　　they are but sins guilt over
With silver dross, whose glistering gloss
　　can them no longer cover.
The best of them would you condemn,
　　and ruine you alone,
Although you were from faults so clear,
　　that other you had none.

Prov. 26:23
Mat. 23:27

Your Gold is brass, your silver dross,
　　your righteousness is sin:
And think you by such honesty
　　eternal life to win?
You much mistake, if for its sake
　　you dream of acceptation;
Whereas the same deserveth shame,
　　and meriteth Damnation.

Prov. 15:8
Rom. 3:20

*Those that
pretend want of
opportunity
to repent.*
Prov. 27:1
Jam. 4:13

A wond'rous Crowd then 'gan aloud,
    thus for themselves to say,
We did intend, Lord to amend,
    and to reform our way:
Our true intent was to repent,
    and make our peace with thee;
But sudden death stopping our breath,
    left us no libertie.

Short was our time, for in his prime
    our youthful flow'r was cropt:
We dy'd in youth, before full growth,
    so was our purpose stopt.
Let our good will to turn from ill,
    and sin to have forsaken,
Accepted be, O Lord, by thee,
    and in good part be taken.

*Are confuted
and Convinced*
Eccles. 12:1
Rev. 2:21

To whom the Judge: where you alledge
    the shortness of the space,
That from your birth you liv'd on earth,
    to compass saving Grace:
It was Free grace that any space
    was given you at all
To turn from evil, defie the Devil,
    and upon God to call.

Luk. 13:24
2 Cor. 6:2
Heb. 3:7, 8, 9

One day, one week, wherein to seek
    God's face with all your hearts,
A favour was that far did pass
    the best of your deserts.
You had a season, what was your reason
    such precious hours to waste?
What could you find, what could you mind
    that was of greater haste?

Could you find time for vain pastime,
    for loose licentious mirth?
For fruitless toyes, and fading joyes   *Eccles.* 11:9
    that perish in the birth?   *Luk.* 14:18, 19,
Had you good leasure for carnal Pleasure,   20
    in dayes of health and youth?
And yet no space to seek God's face,
    and turn to him in truth?

In younger years, beyond your fears,   *Amos* 6:3 *to* 6
    what if you were surprised?
You put away the evil day,   *Eph.* 5:16
    and of long life devised.   *Luk.* 19:42
You oft were told, and might behold,
    that Death no Age doth spare;
Why then did you your time foreslow,
    and slight your Souls welfare?

Had your intent been to repent,
    and had you it desir'd,
There would have been endeavours seen,   *Luk.* 13:24, 25
    before your time expir'd.   *&c.*
God makes no treasure, nor hath he pleasure,   *Phil.* 2:12
    in idle purposes:
Such fair pretences are foul offences,
    and cloaks for wickedness.

Then were brought in, and charg'd with sin,
    another Company,
Who by Petition obtain'd permission,   *Some plead*
    to make Apology: *Examples of their*
They argued, We were misled,   *betters.*
    as is well known to thee,   *Mat.* 18:7
By their Example, that had more ample
    abilities than we:

John 7:48   Such as profest they did detest,
    and hate each wicked way:
Whose seeming grace whilst we did trace,
    our Souls were led astray.
When men of Parts, Learning and Arts,
    Professing Piety,
Did thus and thus, it seem'd to us
    we might take liberty.

Who are told that   The Judge replies, I gave you eyes,
Examples are   and light to see your way,
no Rules.   Which had you lov'd, and well improv'd
Psal. 19: 8, 11   you had not gone astray.
Exo. 23:2
Psal. 50:17,18   My Word was pure, the Rule was sure,
    why did you it forsake,
Or thereon trample, and mens example
    your Directory make?

This you well knew, that God is true
    and that most men are liars,
2 *Tim.* 3:5   In word professing holiness,
    in deed thereof deniers.
O simple fools! that having Rules
    your lives to regulate,
Would then refuse, and rather chuse
    vile men to imitate.

They urge that   But Lord, say they, we went astray,
they were misled by   and did more wickedlie,
godly mens   By means of those whom thou hast chose
Examples   Salvation heirs to be.
But all their shifts
turn to their greater   To whom the Judge: What you alledge,
shame.   doth nothing help the case;
1 *Cor.* 11   But makes appear how vile you were,
    and rend'reth you more base.

38

You understood that what was good,
  was to be followed,
And that you ought that which was naught
  to have relinquished.
Contrariwayes, it was your guise,   *Phil.* 4:8
  only to imitate
Good mens defects, and their neglects
  that were regenerate.

≺ 120 ≻

But to express their holiness,
  or imitate their grace,
You little car'd, nor once prepar'd   Psal. 32:5
  your hearts to seek my face.   2 Chro. 32:26
They did repent, and truly rent   *Mat.* 26:75
  their hearts for all known sin: Prov. 1:24, 25
You did offend, but not amend,
  to follow them therein.

≺ 121 ≻

We had thy Word, say some, O Lord,   *Some plead*
  but wiser men than we   *the Scriptures*
Could never yet interpret it,   *darkness. And*
  but alway disagree.   *difference amongst*
How could we fools be led by Rules,   *Interpreters.*
  so far beyond our ken,   2 Pet. 3:16
Which to explain did so much pain,
  and puzzle wisest men?

≺ 122 ≻

Was all my word abstruse and hard?   *They are confuted.*
  the Judge then answered: Pro. 14:6
It did contain much truth so plain,   *Isa.* 35:8
  you might have run and read,   *Hos.* 8:12
But what was hard you never car'd
  to know nor studied,
And things that were most plain and clear
  you never practised.

39

Mat. 11:25
The Mystery of Pietie
God unto Babes reveals,
When to the wise he it denies,
and from the world conceals.

Prov. 2:3, 4, 5
If to fulfil Gods holy will
had seemed good to you,
You would have sought light as you ought,
and done the good you knew.

Others the fear of
Persecution.
Acts 28:22
Then came in view another Crew,
and 'gan to make their pleas.
Amongst the rest, some of the best
had such poor shifts as these:
Thou know'st right well, who all canst tell
we liv'd amongst thy foes,
Who the Renate did sorely hate,
and goodness much oppose.

John 12:42, 43
We holiness durst not profess,
fearing to be forlorn
Of all our friends, and for amends
to be the wickeds scorn.
We knew their anger would much endanger
our lives, and our estates:
Therefore for fear we durst appear
no better than our mates.

They are
answered.
Luk. 12:4,5
Isa. 51:12,13
To whom the Lord returns this word:
O wonderful deceits!
To cast off aw of Gods strict Law,
and fear mens wrath and threats.
To fear hell-fire and Gods fierce ire
less than the rage of men,
As if Gods wrath, could do less scath
than wrath of bretheren.

To use such strife, a temporal life,
  to rescue and secure,
And be so blind as not to mind
  that life that will endure:
This was your case, who carnal peace
  more than true joyes did favour;
Who fed on dust, clave to your lust,
  and spurned at my favour.

To please your kin, mens love to win,   *Luk.* 9:23, 24, 25
  to flow in worldly wealth,   *Chap.* 16:25
To save your skin, these things have bin
  more than Eternal health.
You had your choice, wherein rejoyce,
  it was your portion,
For which you chose your Souls t'expose
  unto perdition.

Who did not hate friends, life, and state,
  with all things else for me,   *Luk.* 9:26
And all forsake, and's Cross up-take, *Prov.* 8:36
  shall never happy be.   *John* 3:19, 20
Well worthy they to dye for ay,
  who death then life had rather:
Death is their due, that so value
  the friendship of my Father.

Others Argue, and not a few,   *Others plead for*
  is not God gracious?   *Pardon both from*
His Equity and Clemency   *Gods mercy and*
  are they not marvellous?   *justice.*
Thus we believ'd; are we deceiv'd? *Psal.* 78:38
  cannot his mercy great,
(As hath been told to us of old)
  asswage his angers heat?

2 Kings 14:26

How can it be that God should see
    his Creatures endless pain,
Or hear the groans and rueful moans,
    and still his wrath retain?
Can it agree with Equitie?
    can mercy have the heart
To recompence few years offence
    with Everlasting smart?

Can God delight in such a sight
    as sinners misery?
Or what great good can this our blood
    bring unto the most High?

Psal. 30:9
Mic. 7:18

Oh, thou that dost thy Glory most
    in pard'ning sin display!
Lord, might it please thee to release,
    and pardon us this day?

Unto thy Name more glorious fame
    would not such mercy bring?
Would not it raise thine endless praise,
    more than our suffering?
With that they cease, holding their peace,
    but cease not still to weep;
Grief ministers a flood of tears,
    in which their words do steep.

But all too late, grief's out of date,
    when life is at an end.
The glorious King thus answering,
    all to his voice attend:

They answered.

God gracious is, quoth he, like his
    no mercy can be found;
His Equity and Clemency
    to sinners do abound.

42

As may appear by those that here
   are plac'd at my right hand;
Whose stripes I bore, and clear'd the score,
   that they might quitted stand.
For surely none, but God alone,
   whose Grace transcends mens thought,
For such as those that were his foes
   like wonders would have wrought.

*Mercy that now
shines forth in the
vessels of Mercy.*
Mic. 7:18
Rom. 9:23

And none but he such lenitee
   and patience would have shown
To you so long, who did him wrong,
   and pull'd his judgments down.
How long a space (O stiff neck'd race)
   did patience you afford?
How oft did love you gently move,
   to turn unto the Lord?

*Did also long wait
upon such as
abused it.*
Rom. 2:4
Hos. 11:4

With Cords of love God often strove
   your stubborn hearts to tame:
Nevertheless your wickedness,
   did still resist the same.
If now at last Mercy be past
   from you for evermore,
And Justice come in Mercies room,
   yet grudge you not therefore.

Luk. 13:34
*The day of Grace
now past.*

If into wrath God turned hath
   his long long suffering,
And now for love you vengeance prove,
   it is an equal thing.
Your waxing worse, hath stopt the course
   of wonted Clemency:
Mercy refus'd, and Grace misus'd,
   call for severity.

Luk. 19:42, 43
Jude 4

Rom. 2:5, 6
Isa. 1:24
Amos 2:13
Gen. 18:25

It's now high time that ev'ry Crime
 be brought to punishment:
Wrath long contain'd, and oft restrain'd,
 at last must have a vent:
Justice severe cannot forbear
 to plague sin any longer,
But must inflict with hand most strict
 mischief upon the wronger.

Mat. 25:3, 11,
12
Prov. 1:28, 29,
30

In vain do they for Mercy pray,
 the season being past,
Who had no care to get a share
 therein, while time did last.
The man whose ear refus'd to hear
 the voice of Wisdoms cry,
Earn'd this reward, that none regard
 him in his misery.

Isa. 5:18, 19
Gen. 2:17
Rom. 2:8, 9

It doth agree with equity,
 and with Gods holy Law,
That those should dye eternally
 that death upon them draw.
The Soul that sins damnation wins,
 for so the Law ordains;
Which Law is just, and therefore must
 such suffer endless pain.

Rom. 6:23
2 Thess. 1:8, 9

Eternal smart is the desert,
 ev'n of the least offence;
Then wonder not if I allot
 to you this Recompence:
But wonder more, that since so sore
 and lasting plagues are due
To every sin, you liv'd therein,
 who well the danger knew.

◄ 143 ►

God hath no joy to crush or 'stroy,
   and ruine wretched wights,
But to display the glorious Ray
   of Justice he delights.
To manifest he doth detest,
   and throughly hate all sin,
By plaguing it as is most fit,
   this shall him glory win.

Ezek. 33:11
Exod. 34:7
& 14:17
Rom. 9,22

◄ 144 ►

Then at the Bar arraigned are
   an impudenter sort,
Who to evade the guilt that's laid
   upon them, thus retort;
How could we cease thus to transgress?
   how could we Hell avoid,
Whom Gods Decree shut out from thee,
   and sign'd to be destroy'd?

*Some pretend they
were shut out from
Heaven by Gods
Decree.*
Rom. 9:18,19

◄ 145 ►

Whom God ordains to endless pains,
   by Law unalterable,
Repentance true, Obedience new,
   to save such are unable:
Sorrow for sin, no good can win,
   to such as are rejected;
Ne can they grieve, nor yet believe,
   that never were elected.

Heb. 22:17
Rom. 11:7, 8

◄ 146 ►

Of Man's fall'n Race, who can true Grace,
   or Holiness obtain?
Who can convert or change his heart,
   if God withhold the same?
Had we apply'd our selves, and try'd
   as much as who did most
God's love to gain, our busie pain
   and labour had been lost.

*Their pleas
taken off.*
Luk. 13:27
2 *Pet.* 1:9,10
compared with
Mat. 19:6

Christ readily makes this Reply,
　　I damn you not because
You are rejected, or not elected,
　　but you have broke my Laws:
It is but vain your wits to strain,
　　the end and means to sever:
Men fondly seek to part or break
　　what God hath link'd together.

Acts 3:19
& 16:31
* 1 *Sam.* 2:15
John 3:19
Joh. 5:40
2 *Thes.* 2:11,12

Whom God will save, such he will have,
　　the means of life to use:
Whom he'll pass by, shall chuse to dy,
　　and ways of life refuse.
He that fore-sees, and foredecrees,
　　in wisdom order'd has,
That man's free-will electing ill,
　　shall bring his will to pass.

Ezek. 33:11,12,
13
Luk. 13:34
Prov. 8:33,36

High God's Decree, as it is free,
　　so doth it none compel
Against their will to good or ill,
　　it forceth none to Hell.
They have their wish whose Souls perish
　　with Torments in Hell-fire,
Who rather chose their Souls to lose,
　　than leave a loose desire.

Gen. 2:17
Mat. 25:41,42
Ezek. 18:20

God did ordain sinners to pain
　　and I to Hell send none,
But such as swerv'd, and have deserv'd
　　destruction as their own,
His pleasure is, that none from bliss
　　and endless happiness
Be barr'd, but such as wrong'd him much
　　by wilful wickedness.

You, sinful Crew, no other knew
 but you might be elect;
Why did you then your selves condemn?   *2 Pet.* 1:10
 why did you me reject?   *Acts* 13:46
Where was your strife to gain that life   *Luk.* 13:24
 which lasteth evermore?
You never knock'd, yet say God lock'd
 against you Heav'ns door.

'Twas no vain task to knock, to ask,   *Mat.* 7:7, 8
 whilst life continued.
Whoever sought heav'n as he ought,
 and seeking perished?
The lowly meek who truly seek   *Gal.* 5:22, 23
 for Christ, and for Salvation,
There's no Decree whereby such be
 ordain'd to Condemnation.

You argue then: But abject men,
 whom God resolves to spill,
Cannot repent, nor their hearts rent;
 ne can they change their will.
Not for his *Can* is any man
 adjudged unto Hell:
But for his *Will* to do what's ill,   *John* 3:19
 and nilling to do well.

I often stood tend'ring my Blood
 to wash away your guilt:
And eke my Spright to frame you right,
 lest your Souls should be spilt.
But you vile Race, rejected Grace,   *John* 5:40
 when Grace was freely proffer'd:
No changed heart, no heav'nly part
 would you, when it was offer'd.

Who wilfully the Remedy,
    and means of life contemned,
Cause have the same themselves to blame,
    if now they be condemned.

John 15:22.24
Heb. 2:3
Isa. 66:3,4

You have your selves, you and none else,
    your selves have done to dy.
You chose the way to your decay,
    and perisht wilfully.

These words appall and daunt them all;
    dismai'd, and all amort,
Like stocks they stand at Christ's left-hand,
    and dare no more retort.
Then were brought near with trembling fear,
    a number numberless
Of blind Heathen, and bruitish men,
    that did Gods Laws transgress.

Heathen men plead
want of the
written Word.

Whose wicked ways Christ open layes,
    and makes their sins appear,
They making pleas their case to ease,
    if not themselves to clear.
Thy written Word (say they) good Lord,
    we never did enjoy:
We nor refus'd, nor it abus'd;
    Oh, do not us destroy!

Mat. 11:22
Luk. 12:48

You ne'r abus'd, nor yet refus'd
    my written Word, you plead,
That's true (quoth he) therefore shall ye
    the less be punished.
You shall not smart for any part
    of other mens offence,
But for your own transgression
    receive due recompence.

But we were blind, say they, in mind,
   too dim was Natures Light,
Our only guide, as hath been try'd
   to bring us to the sight
Of our estate degenerate,
   and curst by *Adam's* Fall;
How we were born and lay forlorn
   in bondage and in thrall.

1 Cor. 1:21
*And insufficiency
of the Light of
Nature.*

We did not know a Christ till now,
   nor how faln man be saved,
Else would we not, right well we wot,
   have so our selves behaved.
We should have mourn'd, we should have turn'd
   from sin at thy Reproof,
And been more wise through thy advice,
   for our own Souls behoof.

Mat. 11:21

But Natures Light shin'd not so bright
   to teach us the right way:
We might have lov'd it, and well improv'd
   and yet have gone astray.
The Judge most High makes this Reply,
   you ignorance pretend,
Dimness of sight, and want of light
   your course Heav'nward to bend.

*They are
answered.*

How came your mind to be so blind?
   I once you knowledge gave,
Clearness of sight, and judgment right;
   who did the same deprave?
If to your cost you have it lost,
   and quite defac'd the same;
Your own desert hath caus'd the smart,
   you ought not me to blame.

Gen. 1:27
Eccles. 7:29
Hos. 13:9

Mat. 11:25
compard with
20 & 15
Your selves into a pit of woe,
 your own transgression led:
If I to none my Grace had shown,
 who had been injured?
If to a few, and not to you,
 I shew'd a way of life,
My Grace so free, you clearly see,
 gives you no ground of strife.

'Tis vain to tell, you wot full well,
 if you in time had known
Your Misery and Remedy,
 your actions had it shown.
Rom. 1:20, 21, 22 You, sinful Crew, have not been true
 unto the Light of Nature,
Nor done the good you understood,
 nor owned your Creator.

He that the Light, because 'tis Light,
 hath used to despize,
Rom. 2:12, 15
& 1:32
Mat. 12:41
*Reprobate Infants
plead for themselves*
Rev. 20:12, 15
Compared with
Rom. 5:12, 14
& 9:11, 13 Would not the Light shining more bright,
 be likely for to prize.
If you had lov'd, and well improv'd
 your knowledge and dim sight,
Herein your pain had not been vain,
 your plagues had been more light.

Then to the Bar, all they drew near
 who dy'd in Infancy,
And never had or good or bad
 effected pers'nally,
But from the womb unto the tomb
 were straightway carried,
(Or at the last e're they transgrest)
 who thus began to plead:

◄ 167 ►

If for our own transgression,
   or disobedience,
We here did stand at thy left-hand
   just were the Recompence:
But *Adam's* guilt our souls hath spilt,
   his fault is charg'd on us;
And that alone hath overthrown,
   and utterly undone us.

Ezek. 18:2

◄ 168 ►

Not we, but he, ate of the Tree,
   whose fruit was interdicted:
Yet on us all of his sad Fall,
   the punishment's inflicted.
How could we sin that had not been,
   or how is his sin our,
Without consent, which to prevent,
   we never had a pow'r?

◄ 169 ►

O great Creator, why was our Nature
   depraved and forlorn?
Why so defil'd, and made so vild
   whilst we were yet unborn?
If it be just, and needs we must
   transgressors reck'ned be,
Thy Mercy, Lord, to us afford,
   which sinners hath set free.

Psal. 51:5

◄ 170 ►

Behold we see *Adam* set free,
   and sav'd from his trespass,
Whose sinful Fall hath split us all,
   and brought us to this pass.
Canst thou deny us once to try,
   or Grace to us to tender,
When he finds grace before thy face,
   that was the chief offender?

51

Their Argument
taken off.
Ezek. 18:20
Rom. 5:12,19

Then answered the Judge most dread,
   God doth such doom forbid,
That men should dye eternally
   for what they never did.
But what you call old *Adam's* Fall,
   and only his Trespass,
You call amiss to call it his,
   both his and yours it was.

He was design'd of all Mankind
   to be a publick Head,
A common Root, whence all should shoot,
   and stood in all their stead.

1 *Cor.* 15:48,49 He stood and fell, did ill or well,
   not for himself alone,
But for you all, who now his Fall,
   and trespass would disown.

If he had stood, then all his brood
   had been established
In Gods true love, never to move,
   nor once awry to tread:
Then all his Race, my Father's Grace,
   should have enjoy'd for ever,
And wicked Sprights by subtile sleights
   could them have harmed never.

Would you have griev'd to have receiv'd
   through *Adam* so much good,
As had been your for evermore,
   if he at first had stood?
Would you have said, we ne'r obey'd,
   nor did thy Laws regard;
It ill befits with benefits,
   us, Lord, so to reward?

Since then to share in his welfare,
   you could have been content,
You may with reason share in his treason,
   and in the punishment.
Hence you were born in state forlorn,   *Rom.* 5:12
   with Natures so depraved: *Psa.* 51:5
Death was your due, because that you   *Gen.* 5:3
   had thus your selves behaved.

You think if we had been as he,   *Mat.* 23:30,
   whom God did so betrust,   31
We to our cost would ne're have lost
   all for a paltry Lust.
Had you been made in *Adam's* stead,
   you would like things have wrought,
And so into the self-same wo,
   your selves and yours have brought.

I may deny you once to try,   *Rom.* 9:15, 18
   or Grace to you to tender,   *The free gift.*
Though he finds Grace before my face, *Rom.* 5:15
   who was the chief offender:
Else should my Grace cease to be Grace;
   for it should not be free,
If to release whom I should please,
   I have no libertee.

If upon one what's due to none
   I frankly shall bestow,
And on the rest shall not think best,
   compassions skirts to throw,
Whom injure I? will you envy,
   and grudge at others weal?
Or me accuse, who do refuse
   your selves to help and heal?

53

,

Mat. 20:15

Am I alone of what's my own,
   no Master or no Lord?
Or if I am, how can you claim
   what I to some afford?
Will you demand Grace at my hand,
   and challenge what is mine?
Will you teach me whom to set free,
   and thus my Grace confine?

Psa. 58:3
Ro. 6:23
Gal. 3:10
Rom. 8:29, 30
&*11:7
Rev. 21:27
Luk. 12:48

You sinners are, and such a share
   as sinners may expect,
Such you shall have; for I do save
   none but mine own Elect.
Yet to compare your sin with their,
   who liv'd a longer time,
I do confess yours is much less,
   though every sin's a crime.

Mat. 11:22
*The wicked all
convinced and
put to silence.*
Ro. 3:19
Mat. 22:12

A crime it is, therefore in bliss
   you may not hope to dwell;
But unto you I shall allow
   the easiest room in Hell.
The glorious King thus answering,
   they cease, and plead no longer:
Their Consciences must needs confess
   his Reasons are the stronger.

*Behold the
formidable estate
of all the ungodly,
as they stand
hopeless &
helpless before an
impartial Judge,
expecting their
final Sentence.*
Rev. 6:16,17

Thus all mens Pleas the Judge with ease
   doth answer and confute,
Until that all, both great and small,
   are silenced and mute.
Vain hopes are cropt, all mouths are stopt,
   sinners have nought to say,
But that 'tis just, and equal most
   they should be damn'd for ay.

Now what remains, but that to pains
   and everlasting smart,
Christ should condemn the Sons of men,
   which is their just desert;
Oh, rueful plights of sinful wights!
   Oh wretches all forlorn:
'T had happy been they ne're had seen
   the Sun, or not been born.

Yea, now it would be good they could
   themselves annihilate,
And cease to be, themselves to free
   from such a fearful state.
Oh happy Dogs, and Swine, and Frogs:
   yea Serpents generation,
Who do not fear this doom to hear,
   and sentence of Damnation!

This is their state so desperate: *Psa.* 139:2,3,4
   their sins are fully known; *Eccl.* 12:14
Their vanities and villanies
   before the world are shown.
As they are gross and impious,
   so are their numbers more
Than motes i'th' Air, or then their hair,
   or sands upon the shore.

Divine Justice offended is
   and Satisfaction claimeth:
God's wrathful ire kindled like fire,
   against them fiercely flameth.
Their Judge severe doth quite cashier
   and all their Pleas off take, *Mat.* 25:45
That never a man, or dare, or can
   a further Answer make.

Mat. 22:12
Rom. 2:5,6
Luk. 19:42

Their mouths are shut, each man is put
   to silence and to shame:
Nor have they ought within their thought,
   Christ's Justice for to blame.
The Judge is just, and plague them must,
   nor will he mercy shew
(For Mercies day is past away)
   to any of this Crew.

Mat. 28:18
Psal. 139:7

The Judge is strong, doers of wrong
   cannot his power withstand:
None can by flight run out of sight,
   nor scape out of his hand.
Sad is their state: for Advocate
   to plead their Cause there's none:
None to prevent their punishment,
   or misery bemone.

O dismal day! whither shall they
   for help and succour flee?
To God above, with hopes to move
   their greatest Enemee:
His wrath is great, whose burning heat

Isa. 33:14
Psal. 11:6
Numb. 23:19

   no floods of tears can slake:
His word stands fast, that they be cast
   into the burning Lake.

To Christ their Judge, he doth adjudge
   them to the Pit of Sorrow;

Matt. 25:41

Nor will he hear, or cry, or tear,
   nor respite them one morrow.

Matt. 25:10,
11,12

To Heav'n alas, they cannot pass,
   it is against them shut;
To enter there (O heavy cheer)
   they out of hopes are put.

Unto their Treasures, or to their Pleasures,   *Luk.* 12:20
    all these have them forsaken: *Psal.* 49:7, 17
Had they full Coffers to make large offers,
    their Gold would not be taken
Unto the place where whilome was
    their Birth and Education?   *Deut.* 32:2
Lo! Christ begins for their great sins
    to fire the Earths Foundation:

And by and by the flaming Sky   2 *Pet.* 3:10
    shall drop like molten Lead
About their ears, t'increase their fears,
    and aggravate their dread.
To Angels good that ever stood
    in their integrity,
Should they betake themselves, and make
    their sute incessantly?

They neither skill, nor do they will   *Mat.* 13:41,
    to work them any ease: 42
They will not mourn to see them burn,
    nor beg for their release.
To wicked men, their bretheren
    in sin and wickedness,
Should they make mone? their case is one,
    they're in the same distress.   *Rev* 20:13,
                                 15

Ah, cold comfort, and mean support
    from such like Comforters!
Ah, little joy of Company,
    and fellow-sufferers!
Such shall increase their hearts disease,   *Luk.* 16:28
    and add unto their woe,
Because that they brought to decay
    themselves and many moe.

Unto the Saints with sad complaints
    should they themselves apply?
Rev. 21:4   They're not dejected, nor ought affected
    with all their misery.
Friends stand aloof, and make no proof
    what Prayers or Tears can do:
Psal. 58:10   Your godly friends are now more friends
    to Christ than unto you.

◄ 196 ►

Where tender love mens hearts did move
    unto a sympathy,
And bearing part of others smart
    in their anxiety;
1 *Cor.* 6:2   Now such compassion is out of fashion,
    and wholly laid aside:
No Friends so near, but Saints to hear
    their Sentence can abide.

◄ 197 ►

One natural Brother beholds another
    in this astonied fit,
Compare   Yet sorrows not thereat a jot,
Prov. 1:26 *with*   nor pitties him a whit.
1 *Joh.* 3:2 &*
2 *Cor.* 5:16   The godly wife conceives no grief,
    nor can she shed a tear
For the sad state of her dear Mate,
    when she his doom doth hear.

◄ 198 ►

He that was erst a Husband pierc't
    with sense of Wives distress,
Whose tender heart did bear a part
    of all her grievances,
Shall mourn no more as heretofore
    because of her ill plight;
Although he see her now to be
    a damn'd forsaken wight.

The tender Mother will own no other
   of all her numerous brood,
But such as stand at Christ's right hand
   acquitted through his Blood.
The pious Father had now much rather   *Luk.* 16:25
   his graceless Son should ly
In Hell with Devils, for all his evils
   burning eternally,

Then God most high should injury,
   by sparing him sustain;   *Psal.* 58:10
And doth rejoyce to hear Christ's voice
   adjudging him to pain;
Who having all, both great and small,
   convinc'd and silenced,
Did then proceed their Doom to read,
   and thus it uttered:

Ye sinful wights, and cursed sprights,   The Judge
   that work Iniquity,   pronounceth the
Depart together from me for ever   Sentence of
   to endless Misery;   condemnation.
Your portion take in yonder Lake,   *Mat.* 25:41
   where Fire and Brimstone flameth:
Suffer the smart, which your desert
   as it's due wages claimeth.

Oh piercing words more sharp than swords!
   what, to depart from *Thee,*
Whose face before for evermore   *The terrour of it.*
   the best of Pleasures be!
What? to depart (unto our smart)
   from thee *Eternally:*
To be for aye banish'd away,
   with *Devils* company!

59

What? to be sent to *Punishment*,
 and flames of *Burning Fire*,
To be surrounded, and eke confounded
 with Gods *Revengful ire*.
What? to abide, not for a tide
 these Torments, but for *Ever:*
To be released, or to be eased,
 not after years, but *Never*.

Oh, *fearful Doom*! now there's no room
 for hope or help at all:
Sentence is past which aye shall last,
 Christ will not it recall.
There might you hear them rent and tear
 the Air with their out-cries:
The hideous noise of their sad voice
 ascendeth to the Skies.

Luk. 13:28 They wring their hands, their caitiff-hands
 and gnash their teeth for terrour;
They cry, they roar for anguish sore,
 and gnaw their tongues for horrour.
But get away without delay,
 Christ pitties not your cry:
Prov. 1:26 Depart to Hell, there may you yell,
 and roar Eternally.

It is put in
Execution. That word, *Depart*, maugre their heart,
 drives every wicked one,
With mighty pow'r, the self-same hour,
 far from the Judge's Throne.
Mat. 25:46 Away they're chaste by the strong blast
 of his Death-threatning mouth:
They flee full fast, as if in haste,
 although they be full loath.

≺ 207 ≻

As chaff that's dry, and dust doth fly
   before the Northern wind:
Right so are they chased away,
   and can no Refuge find.
They hasten to the Pit of Wo,
   guarded by Angels stout;   *Matt.* 13:41, 42
Who to fulfil Christ's holy will,
   attend this wicked Rout.

≺ 208 ≻

Whom having brought, as they are taught,   *HELL.*
   unto the brink of Hell,   *Mat.* 25:30
(That dismal place far from Christ's face,   *Mark.* 9:43
   where Death and Darkness dwell: *Isa.* 30:33
Where Gods fierce Ire kindleth the fire,   *Rev.* 21:8
   and vengeance feeds the flame
With piles of Wood, and Brimstone Flood,
   that none can quench the same,)

≺ 209 ≻

With Iron bands they bind their hands,   *Wicked Men*
   and cursed feet together,   *and Devils cast into*
And cast them all, both great and small,   *it for ever.*
   into that Lake for ever.   *Mat.* 22:13 &
Where day and night, without respite,   25:46
   they wail, and cry, and howl
For tort'ring pain, which they sustain
   in Body and in Soul.

≺ 210 ≻

For day and night, in their despight,   *Rev.* 14:10, 11
   their torments smoak ascendeth.
Their pain and grief have no relief,
   their anguish never endeth.
There must they ly, and never dy,
   though dying every day:
There must they dying ever ly,
   and not consume away.

61

Dy fain they would, if dy they could,
   but Death will not be had;
God's direful wrath their bodies hath
   for ev'r Immortal made.
They live to ly in misery,
   and bear eternal wo;
And live they must whilst God is just,
   that he may plague them so.

The unsufferable
torments of the
damned.
Luk. 16:24
Jude 7

But who can tell the plagues of Hell,
   and torments exquisite?
Who can relate their dismal state,
   and terrours infinite?
Who fare the best, and feel the least,
   yet feel that punishment
Whereby to nought they should be brought,
   if God did not prevent.

The least degree of miserie
   there felt's incomparable,
The lightest pain they there sustain
   more than intolerable.

Isa. 33:14
Mark 9:43, 44

But God's great pow'r from hour to hour
   upholds them in the fire,
That they shall not consume a jot,
   nor by it's force expire.

But ah, the wo they undergo
   (they more than all besides)
Who had the light, and knew the right,
   yet would not it abide.

Luk. 12:47

The sev'n-fold smart, which to their part,
   and portion doth fall,
Who Christ his Grace would not imbrace,
   nor hearken to his call.

The *Amorites* and *Sodomites*
  although their plagues be sore,   *Mat.* 11:24
Yet find some ease, compar'd to these,
  who feel a great deal more.
Almighty God, whose Iron Rod,
  to smite them never lins,
Doth most declare his Justice rare
  in plaguing these mens sins.

The pain of loss their Souls doth toss,   *Luk.* 16:23, 25
  and wond'rously distress,   *Luk.* 13:28
To think what they have cast away
  by wilful wickedness.
We might have been redeem'd from sin,
  think they, and liv'd above,
Being possest of heav'nly rest,
  and joying in God's love.

But wo, wo, wo our Souls unto!   *Luk.* 13:34
  we would not happy be;
And therefore bear Gods Vengeance here
  to all Eternitee.
Experience and woful sense
  must be our painful teachers
Who n'ould believe, nor credit give,
  unto our faithful Preachers.

Thus shall they ly, and wail, and cry,   *Mark.* 9:44
  tormented, and tormenting   *Rom.* 2:15
Their galled hearts with pois'ned darts
  but now too late repenting.
There let them dwell i'th' Flames of Hell;
  there leave we them to burn,
And back agen unto the men
  whom Christ acquits, return.

The Saints rejoyce
to see Judgment
executed upon the
wicked World.
Ps. 58:10
Rev. 19:1, 2, 3

The Saints behold with courage bold,
    and thankful wonderment,
To see all those that were their foes
    thus sent to punishment:
Then do they sing unto their King
    a Song of endless Praise:
They praise his Name, and do proclaim
    that just are all his ways.

They ascend with
Christ into Heaven
triumphing.
Mat. 25:46
1 *Joh.* 3:2
1 *Cor.* 13:12

Thus with great joy and melody
    to Heav'n they all ascend,
Him there to praise with sweetest layes,
    and Hymns that never end,
Where with long Rest they shall be blest,
    and nought shall them annoy:
Where they shall see as seen they be,
    and whom they love enjoy.

Their Eternal
happiness and
incomparable
Glory there.

O glorious Place! where face to face
    Jehovah may be seen,
By such as were sinners whilere
    and no dark vail between.
Where the Sun shine, and light Divine,
    of Gods bright Countenance,
Doth rest upon them every one,
    with sweetest influence.

Rev. 21:4

O blessed state of the Renate!
    O wondrous Happiness,
To which they're brought, beyond what though
    can reach, or words express!
Griefs water-course, and sorrows sourse,
    are turn'd to joyful streams.
Their old distress and heaviness
    are vanished like dreams.

For God above in arms of love
   doth dearly them embrace,
And fills their sprights with such delights,   *Psal.* 16:11
   and pleasures in his grace;
As shall not fail, nor yet grow stale
   through frequency of use:
Nor do they fear Gods favour there,
   to forfeit by abuse.

For there the Saints are perfect Saints,   *Heb.* 12:23
   and holy ones indeed,
From all the sin that dwelt within
   their mortal bodies freed:
Made Kings and Priests to God through Christs
   dear loves transcendency,   *Rev.* 1:6
There to remain, and there to reign   *&* 22:5
   with him Eternally.

A Short
Discourse on Eternity

≺ 1 ≻
What Mortal man can with his Span
    mete out Eternity?
Or fathom it by depth of Wit,   *Isa.* 57:15
    or strength of Memory?   *Mark.* 3:29
The lofty Sky is not so high,   *Mat.* 25:46
    Hells depth to this is small:
The World so wide is but a stride,
    compared therewithall.

≺ 2 ≻
It is a main great Ocean,
    withouten bank or bound:
A deep Abyss, wherein there is
    no bottom to be found.
This World hath stood now since the Flood,
    four thousand years well near,
And had before endured more
    than sixteen hundred year.

67

But what's the time from the Worlds prime,
    unto this present day,
If we thereby Eternity
    to measure should assay?
The whole duration since the Creation,
    though long, yet is more little,
If placed by Eternity,
    then is the smallest tittle.

Tell every Star both near and far,
    in Heav'ns bright Canopee,
That doth appear throughout the year,
    of high or low degree:
Tell every Tree that thou canst see
    in this vast Wilderness,
Up in the Woods, down by the Floods,
    in thousand miles progress.

The sum is vast, yet not so vast,
    but that thou may'st go on
To multiply the Leaves thereby,
    that hang those Trees upon:
Add thereunto the Drops, that thou
    imaginest to be
In *April* Show'rs, that bring forth Flow'rs,
    and blossoms plenteously:

Number the Fowls and living Souls
    that through the Air do Fly,
The winged Hosts in all their Coasts
    beneath the Starry Sky:
Count all the Grass as thou dost pass
    through many a pasture-land,
And dewy Drops that on the tops
    of Herbs and Plants do stand.

Number the Sand upon the Strand,
    and Atomes of the Air;
And do thy best on Man and Beast,
    to reckon every Hair:
Take all the Dust, if so thou lust,   *2 Thes.* 1:9
    and add to thine Account: *Rev.* 14:11
Yet shall the Years of sinners tears,
    the Number far surmount.

Nought joyn'd to nought can ne're make ought,
    nor Cyphers make a Sum:
Nor things Finite, to infinite
    by multiplying come:
A Cockle-shell may serve as well
    to lade the Ocean dry,
As finite things and Reckonings
    to bound Eternity.

O happy they that live for aye,
    with Christ in Heav'n above!   *1 Thes.* 4:17
Who know withal, that nothing shall   *Rom.* 8:38, 39
    deprive them of his love.
Eternity, Eternity!
    Oh, were it not for thee,
The Saints in bliss and happiness
    could never happy be.

For if they were in any fear,
    that this their joy might cease,   *1 Joh.* 4:18
It would annoy (if not destroy)   *Joh.* 6:35, 40, 51
    and interrupt their peace: *Rev.* 21:4
But being sure it shall endure
    so long as God shall live;
The thoughts of this unto their bliss,
    do full perfection give.

Heb. 12:12

Cheer up, ye Saints, amidst your wants,
    and sorrows many a one,
Lift up the head, shake off all dread,
    and moderate your mone.
Your sufferings and evil things

2 Cor. 4:17
    will suddenly be past;

Psal. 16:11
Your sweet Fruitions, and blessed Visions,
    for evermore shall last.

Lament and mourn you that must burn

Luk. 13:28
    amidst those flaming Seas:

Mat. 25:41, 46
If once you come to such a doom,

Rev. 14:11
    for ever farewel ease.
O sad estate and desperate,
    that never can be mended,
Until Gods Will shall change, or till
    Eternity be ended!

If any one this Question
    shall unto me propound:
What, have the years of sinners tears
    no limits, or no bound?

Mark. 9:43,
44
It kills our heart to think of smart,
    and pains that last for ever;
And hear of fire that shall expire,
    or be extinguish'd never.

I'le Answer make (and let them take
    my words as I intend them:
For this is all the Cordial
    that here I have to lend them)
When Heav'n shall cease to flow with peace
    and all felicity;
Then Hell may cease to be the place
    of Wo and Misery.

When Heav'n is Hell, when Ill is Well,
  when Vertue turns to Vice,
When wrong is Right, when Dark is Light,
  when Nought is of great price:
Then may the years of sinners tears
  and sufferings expire,
And all the hosts of damned ghosts
  escape out of Hell-fire.

When Christ above shall cease to love,
  when God shall cease to reign,
And be no more, as heretofore,
  the Worlds great Sovereign,
Or not be just, or favour lust,
  or in mens sins delight:
Then wicked men (and not till then)
  to Heav'n may take their flight.

When Gods great Power shall be brought lower,
  by forreign Puissance;
Or be decay'd, and weaker made
  through Times continuance:
When drowsiness shall him oppress,
  and lay him fast asleep:
Then sinful men may break their pen,
  and out of Prison creep.

When those in Glory shall be right sory
  they may not change their place,
And wish to dwell with them in Hell,
  never to see Christs face:
Then those in pain may freedom gain,
  and be with Glory dight:
Then Hellish Fiends may be Christs Friends,
  and Heirs of Heaven hight.

Then, Ah poor men! what, not till then?
    No, not an hour before:
For God is just, and therefore must
    torment them evermore.
ETERNITY! ETERNITY!
    thou mak'st hard hearts to bleed:
The thoughts of thee in misery,
    do make men wail indeed.

When they remind what's still behind,
    and ponder this word NEVER,

Mark. 9:43, 44, That they must here be made to bear
45, 46
&c.   Gods Vengeance for EVER:
The thought of this more bitter is,
    then all they feel beside,
Yet what they feel, nor heart of steel,
    nor Flesh of Brass can bide.

21

To lye in wo, and undergo
    the direful pains of Hell,

2 Thes. 1:8, 9 And know withall, that there they shall
    for aye, and ever dwell;
And that they are from rest as far

Mat. 25:46   when fifty thousand year,
Rev. 14:10, 11 Twice told, are spent in punishment,
    as when they first came there.

This, Oh! this makes Hells fiery flakes
    much more intolerable;
This makes frail wights and damned sprights,
    to bear their plagues unable.
This makes men bite, for fell despite,
    their very tongues in twain:
This makes them rore for great horror,
    and trebleth all their pain.

72

A Postscript unto the Reader

And now good Reader, I return again
To talk with thee, who hast been at the pain
To read throughout, and heed what went before;
And unto thee I'le speak a little more.
Give ear, I pray thee, unto what I say,
That God may hear thy voice another day.
Thou hast a Soul, my friend, and so have I,
To save or lose; a Soul that cannot die,
A soul of greater price than Gold and Gems;
A Soul more worth than Crowns and Diadems;
A Soul at first created like its Maker,
And of Gods Image made to be partaker:
Upon the wings of Noblest Faculties,
Taught for to soar above the Starry Skies,
And not to rest, until it understood
It self possessed of the chiefest good.
And since the Fall, thy Soul retaineth still
Those Faculties of Reason and of Will,

73

But Oh, how much deprav'd, and out of frame,
As if they were some others, not the same.
Thine Understanding dismally benighted,
And Reason's eye in Sp'ritual things dim-sighted,
Or else stark blind: Thy Will inclin'd to evil,
And nothing else, a Slave unto the Devil;
That loves to live, and liveth to transgress,
But shuns the way of God and Holiness.
All thine Affections are disordered;
And thou by head-strong Passions are misled.
What need I tell thee of thy crooked way,
And many wicked wand'rings every day?
Or that thine own transgressions are more
In number, than the sands upon the Shore:
Thou art a lump of wickedness become,
And may'st with horrour think upon thy Doom,
Until thy Soul be washed in the flood
Of Christ's most dear, soul-cleansing precious blood.
That, that alone can do away thy sin
Which thou wert born, and hast long lived in.
That, only that, can pacifie Gods wrath,
If apprehended by a lively Faith,
Now whilst the day and means of Grace do last,
Before the opportunity be past.
But if, O man, thou liv'st a Christless creature,
And Death surprize thee in a state of nature,
(As who can tell but that may be thy case)
How wilt thou stand before the Judge's face?
When he shall be reveal'd in flaming fire,
And come to pay ungodly men their hire:
To execute due vengeance upon those
That knew him not, or that have been his foes?
What wilt thou answer unto his demands,
When he requires a reason at thy hands
Of all the things that thou hast said, or done,
Or left undone, or set thine heart upon?

74

When he shall thus with thee expostulate,
What cause hadst thou thy Maker for to hate,
To take up Arms against thy Soveraign,
And Enmity against him to maintain?
What injury hath God Almighty done thee?
What good hath he with-held that might have won thee?
What evil, or injustice, hast thou found
In him, that might unto thine hurt redound?
If neither felt, nor feared injury
Hath moved thee to such hostility;
What made thee then the Fountain to forsake,
And unto broken Pits thy self betake?
What reason hadst thou to dishonour God,
Who thee with Mercies never cease to load?
Because the Lord was good, hast thou been evil,
And taken part against him with the Devil?
For all his cost to pay him with despite,
And all his love with hatred to requite?
Is this the fruit of Gods great patience,
To wax more bold in disobedience?
To kick against the bowels of his Love,
Is this aright his Bounty to improve?
Stand still, ye Heav'ns and be astonished,
That God by man should thus be injured!
Give ear, O Earth, and tremble at the sin
Of those that thine Inhabitants have bin.
But thou, vile wretch, hast added unto all
Thine other faults, and facts so criminal,
The damning sin of wilful unbelief,
Of all Transgressors hadst thou been the chief;
Yet when time was, thou might'st have been set free
From Sin, and Wrath, and punishment by mee.
But thou wouldst not accept of Gospel Grace,
Nor on my terms Eternal Life embrace.
As if that all thy breaches of Gods Law
Were not enough upon thy head to draw

Eternal Wrath: Thou hast despis'd a Saviour,
Rejected me, and trampled on my favour.
How oft have I stood knocking at thy door,
And been denied entrance evermore?
How often hath my Spirit been withstood,
When as I sent him to have done thee good?
Thou hast no need of any one to plead
Thy Cause, or for thy Soul to intercede:
Plead for thy self, if thou hast ought to say,
And pay thy forfeiture without delay.
Behold thou dost ten thousand Talents owe,
Or pay thy Debt, or else to Prison go.
Think, think, O Man, when Christ shall thus unfold
Thy secret guilt, and make thee to behold
The ugly face of all thy sinful errours,
And fill thy Soul with his amazing terrours,
And let thee see the flaming Pit of Hell
(Where all that have no part in him shall dwell)
When he shall thus expostulate the case,
How canst thou bear to look him in the face?
What wilt thou do without an Advocate?
Or plead, when as thy state is desperate?
Dost think to put him off with fair pretences?
Or wilt thou hide and cover thine offences?
Can any thing from him concealed be,
Who doth the hidden things of darkness see?
Art thou of force his Power to withstand?
Canst thou by might escape out of his hand?
Dost thou intend to run out of his sight,
And save thy self from punishment by flight?
Or wilt thou be eternally accurst,
And bide his Vengeance, let him do his worst?
Oh, who can bear his indignations heat?
Or bide the pains of Hell, which are so great?
If then thou neither canst his Wrath endure,
Nor any Ransom after death procure:

If neither Cryes nor Tears can move his heart
To pardon thee, or mittigate thy smart,
But unto Hell thou must perforce be sent
With dismal horrour and astonishment:
Consider, O my Friends, what cause thou hast
With fear and trembling (while as yet thou may'st)
To lay to heart thy sin and misery,
And to make out after the Remedy.
Consider well the greatness of thy danger,
O Child of wrath, and object of Gods anger,
Thou hangest over the Infernal Pit
By one small threed, and car'st thou not a whit?
There's but a step between thy Soul and Death,
Nothing remains but stopping of thy breath,
(Which may be done to morrow, or before)
And then thou art undone for evermore.
Let this awaken thy Security,
And make thee look about thee speedily,
How canst thou rest an hour or sleep a night,
Or in thy Creature-comforts take delight;
Or with vain Toyes thy self forgetfull make
How near thou art unto the burning Lake?
How canst thou live without tormenting fears?
How canst thou hold from weeping floods of tears,
Yea, tears of blood, I might almost have sed,
If such like tears could from thine eyes be shed?
To gain the world what will it profit thee,
And loose thy Soul and self eternallie?
Eternity on one small point dependeth:
The man is lost that this short life mispendeth,
For as the Tree doth fall, right so it lies;
And man continues in what state he dies.
Who happy die, shall happy rise again;
Who cursed die, shall cursed still remain,
If under Sin, and Wrath, Death leaves thee bound,
At Judgment under Wrath thou shalt be found:

77

And then wo, wo that ever thou wert born,
O wretched man, of Heav'n and Earth forlorn!
Consider this, all ye that God forget,
Who all his threatenings at nought do set,
Lest into pieces he begin to tear
Your Souls, and there be no deliverer.
O you that now sing care and fear away,
Think often of the formidable Day,
Wherein the Heavens with a mighty noise,
And with a hideous, heart-confounding voice,
Shall pass away together, being roll'd
As men are wont their garments for to fold;
When th' Elements with fervent heat shall melt,
And living Creatures in the same shall swelt,
And altogether in those Flames expire,
Which set the Earths Foundations on fire.
Oh, what amazement will your hearts be in,
And how will you to curse your selves begin
For all your damned sloth, and negligence,
And unbelief, and gross Impenitence,
When you shall hear that dreadful Sentence past,
That all the wicked into Hell be cast?
What horrour will your Consciences surprise,
When you shall hear the fruitless doleful cries
Of such as are compelled to depart
Unto the place of everlasting smart?
What, when you see the sparks fly out of Hell,
And view the Dungeon where you are to dwell,
Wherein you must eternally remain
In anguish, and intolerable pain?
What, when your hands and feet are bound together,
And you are cast into that Lake for ever?
Then shall you feel the truth of what you hear,
That hellish pains are more than you can bear,
And that those Torments are an hundred fold
More terrible than ever you were told.

Nor speak I this, good Reader, to torment thee
Before the time, but rather to prevent thee
From running head-long to thine own decay,
In such a perillous and deadly way.
We, who have known and felt Jehovah's terrours,
Perswade men to repent them of their errours,
And turn to God in time, e're his Decree
Bring forth, and then there be no Remedee!
If in the night, when thou art fast aleep,
Some friend of thine, that better watch doth keep,
Should see thy house all on a burning flame,
And thee almost inclosed with the same:
If such a friend should break thy door and wake thee,
Or else by force out of the peril take thee:
What? wouldst thou take his kindness in ill part?
Or frown upon him for his good desert?
Such, O my friend, such is thy present state,
And danger, being unregenerate.
Awake, awake, and then thou shalt perceive
Thy peril greater then thou wilt believe.
Lift up thine eyes, and see Gods wrathful ire,
Preparing unextinguishable fire
For all that live and die impenitent.
Awake, awake, O Sinner, and repent,
And quarrel not, because I thus alarm
Thy Soul, to save it from eternal harm.
Perhaps thou harbourest such thoughts as these:
I hope I may enjoy my carnal ease
A little longer, and my self refresh
With those delights that gratifie the flesh,
And yet repent before it be too late,
And get into a comfortable state;
I hope I have yet many years to spend,
And time enough those matters to attend.
Presumptuous heart! Is God engag'd to give
A longer time to such as love to live

79

Like Rebels still, who think to stain his Glory
By wickedness, and after to be sory?
Unto thy lust shall he be made a drudge,
Who thee, and all ungodly men, shall judge?
Canst thou account sin sweet, and yet confess,
That first, or last, it ends in bitterness?
Is sin a thing that must procure thee sorrow?
And wouldst thou dally with't another morrow?
O foolish man, who lovest to enjoy
That which will thee distress, or else destroy!
What gained *Sampson* by his *Delilah?*
What gained *David* by his *Bathsheba?*
The one became a Slave, lost both his eyes,
And made them sport that were his Enemies;
The other penneth, as a certain token
Of Gods displeasure, that his bones were broken,
Besides the woes he after met withal,
To chasten him for that his grievous Fall:
His own Son *Ammon* using crafty wiles,
His Daughter *Thamar* wickedly defiles;
His second Son more beautiful than good,
His hands embreweth in his Brothers Blood:
And by and by aspiring to the Crown,
He strives to pull his gentle Father down:
With hellish rage, him fiercely persecuting,
And bruitishly his Concubines polluting.
Read whoso list, and ponder what he reads,
And he shall find small joy in evil deeds.
Moreover this consider, that the longer
Thou liv'st in sin, thy sin will grow the stronger,
And then it will an harder matter prove,
To leave those wicked haunts that thou dost love.
The Black-moor may as eas'ly change his skin,
As old transgressors leave their wonted sin.
And who can tell what may become of thee,
Or where thy Soul in one days time may be?

We see that Death ner old nor young men spares,
But one and other takes at unawares.
For in a moment, whil'st men Peace do cry,
Destruction seizeth on them suddenly.
Thou who this morning art a lively wight,
May'st be a Corps and damned Ghost ere night.
Oh, dream not then, that it will serve the turn,
Upon thy death bed for thy sins to mourn,
But think how many have been snatcht away,
And had no time for mercy once to pray.
It's just with God Repentance to deny
To such as put it off until they dy,
And late Repentance seldom proveth true,
Which if it fail, thou know'st what must ensue;
For after this short life is at an end,
What is amiss thou never canst amend.
Believe, O man, that to procrastinate,
And put it off until it be too late,
As 'tis thy sin, so is it Satans wile,
Whereby he doth great multitudes beguile.
How many thousands hath this strong delusion
Already brought to ruine and confusion,
Whose Souls are now reserv'd in Iron Chains,
Under thick darkness to eternal pains?
They thought of many years, as thou dost now,
But were deceived quite, and so may'st thou.
Oh, then my friend, while not away thy time,
Nor by rebellion aggravate thy Crime.
Oh put not off Repentance till to morrow,
Adventure not without Gods leave to borrow
Another day to spend upon thy lust,
Lest God (that is most holy, wise, and just)
Denounce in wrath, and to thy terrour say:
This night shall Devils fetch thy Soul away.
Now seek the face of God with all thy heart;
Acknowledge unto him how vile thou art;

81

Tell him thy sins deserve eternal wrath,
And that it is a wonder that he hath
Permitted thee so long to draw thy breath,
Who might have cut thee off by sudden death,
And sent thy Soul into the lowest Pit,
From whence no price should ever ransom it,
And that he may most justly do it still
(Because thou hast deserv'd it) if he will.
Yet also tell him that, if he shall please,
He can forgive thy Sins, and thee release,
And that in Christ his Son he may be just,
And justifie all those that on him trust:
That though thy sins are of a crimson dy,
Yet Christ his Blood can cleanse thee thorowly.
Tell him, that he may make his glorious Name
More wonderful by covering thy shame;
That Mercy may be greatly magnify'd,
And Justice also fully satisfy'd,
If he shall please to own thee in his Son,
Who hath paid dear for Men's Redemption.
Tell him thou hast an unbelieving heart,
Which hindereth thee from coming for a part
In Christ: and that although his terrours aw thee,
Thou canst not come till he be pleas'd to draw thee.
Tell him thou know'st thine heart to be so bad,
And thy condition so exceeding sad,
That though Salvation may be had for nought
Thou canst not come and take, till thou be brought.
Oh beg of him to bow thy stubborn Will
To come to Christ, that he thy lusts may kill.
Look up to Christ for his attractive pow'r,
Which he exerteth in a needful hour;
Who saith, whenas I lifted up shall be,
Then will I draw all sorts of men to me.
O wait upon him with true diligence,
And trembling fear in every Ordinance;

Unto his call earnest attention give,
Whose voice makes deaf men hear, and dead men live.
Thus weep, and mourn, thus hearken, pray and wait,
Till he behold, and pitty thine estate,
Who is more ready to bestow his Grace,
Then thou the same art willing to imbrace;
Yea, he hath Might enough to bring thee home,
Though thou hast neither strength nor will to come.
If he delay to answer thy request,
Know that oft-times he doth it for the best:
Not with intent to drive us from his door,
But for to make us importune him more;
Or else to bring us duly to confess,
And be convinc'd of our unworthiness.
Oh, be not weary then, but persevere
To beg his Grace till he thy suit shall hear:
And leave him not, nor from his foot-stool go,
Till over thee Compassions skirt he throw.
Eternal Life will recompence thy pains,
If found at last, with everlasting gains.
For if the Lord be pleas'd to hear thy cryes,
And to forgive thy great iniquities,
Thou wilt have cause for ever to admire,
And laud his Grace, that granted thy desire.
Then shalt thou find thy labour is not lost:
But that the good obtain'd surmounts the cost.
Nor shalt thou grieve for loss of sinful pleasures,
Exchang'd for heavenly joyes and lasting treasures.
The yoke of Christ, which once thou didst esteem
A tedious yoke, shall then most easie seem.
For why? The love of Christ shall thee constrain
To take delight in that which was thy pain;
The wayes of Wisdom shall be pleasant wayes,
And thou shalt chuse therein to spend thy dayes.
If once thy Soul be brought to such a pass,
O'bless the Lord, and magnifie his Grace.

Thou, that of late hadst reason to be sad,
May'st now rejoyce, and be exceeding glad,
For thy condition is as happy now,
As erst it was disconsolate and low;
Thou art become as rich as whilome poor,
As blessed now, as cursed heretofore;
For being cleansed with Christs precious Blood,
Thou hast an int'rest in the chiefest good:
Gods anger is towards thy Soul appeased,
And in his Christ he is with thee well pleased.
Yea, he doth look upon thee with a mild
And gracious aspect as upon his child;
He is become thy Father and thy Friend,
And will defend thee from the cursed Fiend.
Thou need'st not fear the roaring Lyon's rage,
Since God Almighty doth himself engage
To bear thy Soul in Everlasting Armes,
Above the reach of all destructive harms.
What ever here thy sufferings may be,
Yet from them all the Lord shall rescue thee.
He will preserve thee by his wond'rous might
Unto that rich Inheritance in light.
Oh, sing for joy, all ye regenerate,
Whom Christ hath brought into this blessed state!
O love the Lord, all ye his Sains, who hath
Redeemed you from everlasting wrath:
Who hath by dying made your Souls to live,
And what he dearly bought doth freely give:
Give up your selves to walk in all his wayes,
And study how to live unto his praise.
The time is short you have to serve him here:
The day of your deliv'rance draweth near.
Lift up your heads, ye upright ones in heart,
Who in Christ's purchase have obtain'd a part.
Behold, he rides upon a shining Cloud,
With Angels voice, and Trumpet sounding loud;

He comes to save his folk from all their foes,
And plague the men that Holiness oppose.
So come, Lord Jesus, quickly come we pray:
Yea come, and hasten our Redemption day.

Danity of Danities

A Song of Emptiness

To Fill up the Empty Pages Following

Vain, frail, short liv'd, and miserable Man,
Learn what thou art when thine estate is best:
A restless Wave o'th' troubled Ocean,
A Dream, a lifeless Picture finely drest:

A Wind, a Flower, a Vapour, and a Bubble,
A Wheel that stands not still, a trembling Reed,
A rolling Stone, dry Dust, light Chaff, and Stubble,
A Shadow of Something, but nought indeed.

Learn what deceitful Toyes, and empty things,
This World, and all its best Enjoyments bee:
Out of the Earth no true Contentment springs,
But all things here are vexing Vanitee.

For what is *Beauty*, but a fading Flower?
Or what is *Pleasure*, but the Devils bait,
Whereby he catcheth whom he would devour,
And multitudes of Souls doth ruinate?

87

And what are *Friends* but mortal men, as we?
Whom Death from us may quickly separate;
Or else their hearts may quite estranged be,
And all their love be turned into hate.

And what are *Riches* to be doted on?
Uncertain, fickle, and ensnaring things;
They draw Mens Souls into Perdition,
And when most needed, take them to their wings.

Ah foolish Man! that sets his heart upon
Such empty Shadows, such wild Fowl as these,
That being gotten will be quickly gone,
And whilst they stay increase but his disease.

As in a Dropsie, drinking draughts begets,
The more he drinks, the more he still requires:
So on this World whoso affection sets,
His Wealths encrease encreaseth his desires.

O happy Man, whose portion is above,
Where Floods, where Flames, where Foes cannot bereave hi
Most wretched man, that fixed hath his love
Upon this World, that surely will deceive him!

For, what is *Honour?* What is *Sov'raignty,*
Whereto mens hearts so restlesly aspire?
Whom have they Crowned with Felicity?
When did they ever satisfie desire?

The Ear of Man with hearing is not fill'd:
To see new sights still coveteth the Eye:
The craving Stomack though it may be still'd,
Yet craves again without a new supply.

All Earthly things, man's Cravings answer not,
Whose little heart would all the World contain,
(If all the World should fall to one man's Lot)
And notwithstanding empty still remain.

The *Eastern Conquerour* was said to weep,
When he the *Indian* Ocean did view,
To see his Conquest bounded by the Deep,
And no more Worlds remaining to subdue.

Who would that man in his Enjoyments bless,
Or envy him, or covet his estate,
Whose gettings do augment his greediness,
And make his wishes more intemperate?

Such is the wonted and the common guise
Of those on Earth that bear the greatest Sway:
If with a few the case be otherwise
They seek a Kingdom that abides for ay.

Moreover they, of all the Sons of men,
That Rule, and are in highest places set,
Are most inclin'd to scorn their Bretheren
And God himself (without great grace) forget.

For as the Sun doth blind the gazer's eyes,
That for a time they nought discern aright:
So Honour doth befool and blind the Wise,
And their own Lustre 'reaves them of their sight.

Great are their Dangers, manifold their Cares;
Thro which, whilst others Sleep, they scarcely Nap
And yet are oft surprized unawares,
And fall unweeting into Envies Trap!

The mean Mechanick finds his kindly rest,
All void of fear Sleepeth the Country-Clown,
When greatest Princes often are distrest,
And cannot Sleep upon their Beds of Down.

Could *Strength* or *Valour* men Immortalize,
Could *Wealth* or *Honour* keep them from decay,
There were some cause the same to Idolize,
And give the lye to that which I do say.

But neither can such things themselves endure
Without the hazard of a Change one hour,
Nor such as trust in them can they secure
From dismal dayes, or Deaths prevailing pow'r.

If *Beauty* could the beautiful defend
From Death's dominion, then fair *Absalom*
Had not been brought to such a shameful end:
But fair and foul unto the Grave must come.

If *Wealth* or *Scepters* could Immortal make,
Then wealthy *Croesus*, wherefore art thou dead?
If *Warlike force*, which makes the World to quake,
Then why is *Julius Caesar* perished?

Where are the *Scipio's* Thunder-bolts of War?
Renowned *Pompey*, *Caesars* Enemie?
Stout *Hannibal*, *Romes* Terror known so far?
Great *Alexander*, what's become of thee?

If *Gifts* and *Bribes* Death's favour might but win,
If *Power*, if force, or *Threatnings* might it fray,
All these, and more, had still surviving been:
But all are gone, for Death will have no Nay.

Such is this World with all her Pomp and Glory,
Such are the men whom worldly eyes admire:
Cut down by Time, and now become a Story,
That we might after better things aspire.

Go boast thy self of what thy heart enjoyes,
Vain Man! triumph in all thy worldly Bliss:
Thy best enjoyments are but Trash and Toyes:
Delight thy self in that which worthless is.

Omnia praetereunt praeter amare Deum.

THE TEXT OF THIS EDITION

The Harvard College Library owns a copy of the "Fifth Edition" of Wigglesworth's *The Day of Doom*, printed in Boston in 1701. The text of this, said to be the earliest known complete copy of any American edition, has been followed in this reprint, except for a few changes noted below.

The only earlier versions of *The Day of Doom* extant in complete copies were printed in London, where they must have been produced without the author's supervision, and the editions later than 1701 all appeared after Wigglesworth's death. The 1701 text, therefore, seems most likely to represent his final wishes for the poem.

In reprinting the 1701 edition its punctuation has now and then been amended to make for easier reading, "&" has been printed as "and," except in the marginal notes, and the old long "ſ" has been replaced by the modern "s." The spelling, capitalization, and italicization of the original have been kept, since it is difficult to separate those forms which represent seventeenth century American usage, or were deliberately used by the author, from those which were created by a too hasty typesetter, and since some readers may be interested to see just how *The Day of Doom* confronted its audience in 1701. In a few cases, however, obvious typographical slips in the original have been set right, but all such alterations have been listed here, so that anyone who cares to may reconstruct the original:

PAGE 10, STANZA 3, LINE 1

"Like as of Gold" has been corrected to "Like as of old," which accords with the 7th edition, Boston, 1751.

PAGE 10, STANZA 6, LINE 1

"cush" corrected to "rush," as in the 6th edition, Boston, 1715, and the 7th.

PAGE 14, STANZA 20, MARGINAL NOTE

"*all*" corrected to "*All.*"

PAGE 17, STANZA 32, LINE 2

"where" corrected to "were," as in the 7th edition.

PAGE 24, STANZA 60, LINE 5

"Tslents" corrected to "Talents" as in the 6th and 7th editions.

PAGE 25, STANZA 66, LINE 8

"seath" corrected to "scath" (injury, harm). "Seath" remains in the 6th edition, but is changed to "death" in the 7th. "Scath" is, however, the word obviously required by the sense and rhyme. It is used elsewhere in the poem. See p. 40, stanza 126, l. 7.

PAGE 29, STANZA 81, MARGINAL NOTE

"*hyporites*" corrected to "*hypocrites*" as in the 6th edition.

PAGE 31, STANZA 88, MARGINAL NOTE

"*Psal.* 78, 34, 55," corrected to "*Psal.* 78:34, 35."

PAGE 40, STANZA 125, LINE 7

"dust" corrected to "durst," as in the 7th edition.

PAGE 50, STANZA 163, MARGINAL NOTE

"*Mat.* 1:25" corrected to "*Mat.* 11:25."

PAGE 90, STANZA 4, LINE 2

"than" corrected to "then" as in the 7th edition.

The verses "On the following Work, And It's Author" by "J. Mitchel," which are found in the 1701 edition, have been omitted in this reprint, but everything of Wigglesworth's own in that volume appears here.

EXPLANATORY NOTES

For the most part the style and language of the poems in this volume are simple, and there are few places where elucidatory notes are needed. Now and then an unusual spelling may seem unintelligible, but ordinarily to pronounce the word in question identifies it in spite of the orthography. Therefore the few notes which follow are by no means exhaustive, but are simply explanatory definitions of a few words or phrases which may to some readers prove puzzling.

amort: spiritless, dejected. PAGE 48, STANZA 156.

bare the Bell: took the first place, was chief. PAGE 35, STANZA 104.

chaste: chased. PAGE 60, STANZA 206.

flow in worldly wealth: abound in wealth. PAGE 41, STANZA 128.

foreslow: to lose or spoil by sloth. PAGE 37, STANZA 112.

hight: called, named. PAGE 71, STANZA 18.

lade: bale. PAGE 69, STANZA 8.

last: in the phrase *at the last,* PAGE 50, STANZA 166, seems to mean "latest."

lins: ceases. PAGE 63, STANZA 215.

ne: nor. PAGE 45, STANZA 145; PAGE 47, STANZA 153.

ned: obsolete form of *need.* PAGE 26, STANZA 70.

nilling: not willing. PAGE 47, STANZA 153.

n'ould: would not. (PAGE 63, STANZA 217.)

or . . . or: either . . . or. PAGE 56, STANZA 190.

prove: in the phrase *and now for love you vengeance prove* means experience, so that the phrase means "now instead of love you experience vengeance." PAGE 43, STANZA 138.

Renate: the reborn, the elect, those chosen to salvation. PAGE 40, STANZA 124; PAGE 64, STANZA 222, etc.

rent: often used where modern usage would require "rend." Cf. PAGE 12, STANZA 11.

skill: know how to. PAGE 57, STANZA 193.

swelt: die, perish, or, simply, swelter. PAGE 78, LINE 14.

vild: vile. PAGE 51, STANZA 169.